OCCUPY LOVE by Jerry Alatalo

Copyright 2012 / ISBN-13: 978-1479205097

Printed in the United States of America

Contents.

Thank you God, Great Spirit, Creator, Source. Dedicated to all of our family and friends here and ascended. Dedicated to all of the Spiritual masters here and ascended. Dedicated to all peacemakers here and ascended. We pray that all humanity is in the light. We pray for Love.

Part One. The Physical Realm. Begin.

"The only thing that we can know is that we know nothing and that is the highest flight of human wisdom." Leo Tolstoy (1828-1910) Russian writer

Thank you for reading this collection of ideas. First of all let us pray that there will be something good for you as a result of your taking in these words. For this effort is both for you and for us. There is a theory that says in order for one to learn it helps to teach. We would not characterize this collection as one where the reader is the student while the writer is the teacher. Perhaps the more apt characterization is that the reader is receiving a message shared with the writer. Sharing is that which one does out of a Spirit of giving. We pray that these words are a gift to you.

If after you read these ideas there is any realization on your part that you may have received a gift, then the writer will have succeeded at one of the goals of the work. We all have something in common and that is we all are searchers for truth. Hopefully the ideas here are going to ring true for you. We all have come across various works of art, perhaps a wonderful movie which leaves us profoundly moved and full of hope for mankind. Another example is a work of beautiful music that leaves us breathless, overwhelmingly grateful to have had the opportunity to hear it along with utter appreciation for the artists who created it.

Are not the profoundly moving efforts of others the greatest experience? These are the Creations of our fellow human beings which contain the highest levels of positive Spiritual content, pointing and taking us to a place of Sacred beauty and wonder. Those works which rise to the most elevated levels and bring out the best in us are so much to be treasured. With books they are those that you are so impressed with that you give copies to your family and friends while always having your copy on the bookshelf. These are the books that you read time and again with each reading bringing more.

If this work came to be considered by any of you reading it a "keeper" that would be meeting one of the writer's goals. This would mean that truth was conveyed and meaning was uncovered. That will mean that the reader and the writer have connected in an important way which relates to truth concerning this common experience we call life. Being our first effort at putting together a book of ideas in non-fiction form, we do have as one of our goals to have included ideas which will literally improve the human condition. The effort to improve the human condition on planet Earth, along with the successful manifestation of that effort, was one of the criteria Leo Tolstoy came to believe constituted true art. The other major criteria Tolstoy came to believe needed to be met by a work of art was that it must truly convey the highest Spiritual feeling and thought available on Earth at the time.

If this writer is fortunate enough the work will meet Tolstoy's criteria of giving the reader a sense of the highest Spiritual feeling on Earth. If it results in a literal improvement in the conditions of mankind, Mother Earth, the animal relatives and all of Creation then the writer will have achieved an objective. We have attempted to convey high Spiritual thoughts which contain the potential for mankind's transformation. It would be presumptuous for the writer to attempt to believe any of the ideas in the work relating to Spirit are the highest on Earth. There are men and women living on Earth at this time who have a greater, more comprehensive grasp and understanding of Spirit than the writer. Many have spent a great deal more time and effort working on truth and enlightenment.

Perhaps we will have the opportunity to share thoughts with those men and women who do have the highest possible knowledge of Spirit on Earth in the near future. As one who has only found the internet recently there are probably those of you reading this who have a greater appreciation for all of the available information. We do believe that the internet is a divine gift to humanity. The ability of human beings to truly communicate with their brothers and sisters all around planet Earth is no doubt God given. Without the advent of the internet many millions of men and women would never have been able to communicate. This communication tool is responsible for all of the evolutionary changes we are witnessing.

This book will not be a lengthy one nor is it written for researchers, intellectuals or academics. The ideas are primarily for the average man or woman who does not have the luxury of being able to spend time drilling down on the issues facing humanity in 2012. We are talking about the folks who go to jobs in order to raise their families, pay the mortgages and the bills while putting food on their tables. We are writing for those who are not financially well off but have to struggle and worry about making ends meet. Those who are most affected by the political, financial, ideological and corporate systems that are dominant at this time.

This work is not difficult to read and avoids complexity in order for the information to be accessible to the largest part of the human family. We are attempting to reach the largest possible number of our fellow brothers and sisters so the work must remain within reach and readable. Our target readers are primarily those who have not had access to educational opportunities nor the luxury of high incomes. We have as one goal getting the message out to those that are having a hard time of it these days; that there are those who have not forgotten you and care about you.

For those who have had the opportunities educationally and financially we believe this information also pertains to you. Although the ideas and views are somewhat different than the information provided by mainstream media companies this is not a book meant to entertain. This book's message is meant to uplift humanity and aid with Spiritual knowledge, leading to a world with increases in fairness, justice and mercy. Essentially we are aiming to bring Christ consciousness to as many people on Earth as possible. As we search for Spiritual truth we arrive at points along the way where we add new knowledge to the best philosophies that we are aware of at any given time. The additions continue for the rest of our lifetimes and on into forever.

We would ask forgiveness at the outset for any writings which intentionally or not seem to contain any form of judgment. As the Spiritual masters told us to forgive we would issue a form of blanket forgiveness here for all those who are seemingly criticized or judged. As difficult as it is sometimes to forgive, considering the cruel actions taken by humans against their fellow humans, forgiveness is the only option. As Jesus said, "Forgive them father. They know not what they do." Perhaps these writings will end up in the hands of some who have harmed their brothers and sisters. We would say to them that one can convert to a Love/Spirit directed life at any time.

The sections of the Gnostic writings which contain the idea of keeping truth to oneself resulting in one's death is another reason for this effort. When one understands the Spiritual meaning of Christ's words then there is no other choice but to act accordingly; any truth that we may have come across must be shared with others. In passing, can we imagine the thoughts that came to men and women before the invention of electricity? Before the printed word? These people had no televisions, CD players, books, computers, magazines. Can we imagine the power of thought that these people were able to develop without any distractions? We have all been in power outages where we go somewhat stir crazy with the silence.

Silence was a permanent condition way back then. The people who lived before electricity were in essence having 24/7/365 meditation sessions. It therefore explains why the ancient Spiritual writings have such a depth and richness. It explains why present day men and women appreciate the wisdom found in the centuries old texts and writings. It could perhaps explain the diminishment of thought work which matched the works written before electricity came along. When Gandhi was being praised for the wise words he used he responded that "This wisdom is as old as the hills." So Gandhi studied the ancient texts and history records the results of the knowledge and wisdom he received. There is a tremendous amount of ancient Spiritual writings available to read on the internet.

This work could be considered abstract art similar to that of Pablo Picasso or Jackson Pollock. We have made an effort to stay away from being too esoteric to allow those who have not read a lot on these issues to digest the ideas. The writings could be compared to jazz music similar to that of Miles Davis or Chick Corea and improvisational. We have no master's degree in English. As one who does not have any particular expertise in English, writing, structure or style we are giving it our best shot and hoping the ideas break through. Technical rules of English composition do not interest us so our style of writing may seem to be cruder than writings you are accustomed to. We apologize for any awkwardness you may feel because of this.

We have arrived at the point where the work is divided into two parts. The first part will deal with the world of the physical realm. Topics considered are media and communications, violence and wars, international finance and banking, food problems and genetically modified organisms. These issues are examined as they seem to be those which have the most impact on humanity as a whole at this time. These seem to be the most important areas of concern for mankind. We stress the more easily understood larger points to be made concerning each topic and issue. One could drill down further into these areas but sometimes too much minutiae gets in the way of a personal grasp and understanding of ideas.

The Part One issues and topics are given a basic study which we find sufficient to convey the current and historical states of these human activities. A broad general awareness will be gained concerning these areas and that is all we are after here. Once again our hope is for the largest number of people to begin their awareness of these matters. We will say that the physical realm has some things going on that baffle the mind. When one tries to understand these issues, the reasoning mind definitely is challenged in a large way.

Part Two will contrast Part One's physical realm with writings concerning Spirituality. Ideally the reader will, after looking at physical realm conditions in Part One and discovering that there is an urgent need for solutions, find Spiritual power in Part Two that will be valuable for solutions work. The contrast between the physical realm and the Spiritual realm gives one a more balanced awareness of the totality of life and the creative potential which allows for reasonable efforts to be taken at problem solving.

The sheer volume of information available from researchers and writers on these areas of concern is huge. There are literally millions of books and articles that have been written on each and every one of these topics throughout history. This first time writer on these topics is somewhat awestruck at even attempting to bring an understanding of them to people. At any rate we are alone in the room with a pencil and paper and will give it our best. These are the hurdles all writers face when they make the effort to produce the work. They risk criticism and all that goes with it. It seems that there is a point where the writer simply has no alternative but to go forward and finish the work to the best of their ability.

Given the writer has come to a point where they believe there are some thoughts and ideas of a certain importance which could be beneficial if shared with others, the decision to dare the attempt is made. An analogy would be where a person mentions or suggests something to a family member or friend that the person believes would be of help. Another analogy could be seeing someone unaware of a car about to strike them and another yelling to them to watch out for the car. We understand that these are simple analogies. Who made the rule that the communication of ideas had to be done with a high level of complexity?

One need only to begin reading some of the books written by the great philosophers to know that some are overly complex. Some hold the position that simplicity is a good thing. Some hold the position that there is nothing to be gained by beating a point to death. So we will not attempt to make a grand display of any intellectual prowess or any ability to hang with the "big dogs". This work has one purpose and one purpose only. That purpose is to make life better for all people, Mother Earth, all living things and all of the Creation.

This work is an attempt to communicate to others in such a way that good results on Earth are made visible. Hopefully the words will contain wisdom that ring true to others and will be of help. We hope and pray that the Creator will grant us humility when doing this communicative work so that the highest level of benefit for others will be realized. We pray for all those on Mother Earth who are making similar efforts to help humanity and make life a little better for others. Those who have made and are making efforts to improve the human condition despite the odds deserve our greatest thanks and appreciation.

There is a theory that our thoughts create our reality. If there are any thoughts contained in this work that you think are positive then, if the theory is correct, our combined thinking will manifest the reality of a better world. We remember the words Jesus spoke about having faith the size of a mustard seed. With that small amount of faith one could move a mountain. We are attempting to move mountains here, there is no doubt about it. The question is will we be able to gather enough faith to get the job done. One thing is for certain. The people on Earth will never stop with their efforts, prayers and work to make the world a better place for everyone.

The sum total of humanity's thoughts is called the collective consciousness. For whatever reasons the collective consciousness of humanity is being raised at this time. Perhaps this is the way evolution in the physical realm works; this is what we will learn when we leave this physical realm. The issue at hand while we are in the physical realm is getting as close as humanly possible to the truth of our existence. The work of thinking in order to find truth, of creative thought, is work that involves the risk of having to visit some very dark places. Given the events that we witness as humans on Earth one may come to some conclusions. That sanity is perpetually risked simply by experiencing the world around us.

What one depends on to keep their sanity is the question. Not one serious creative artist or serious human being is exempt from the risk. That awareness allows one to understand the importance of making sure that as many of those one interacts with understand that you are aware of their struggles. This human to human interaction and understanding is important for all people; none of us can go it alone in this life. You are able to create the mutual understanding because you are both aware of the struggles we all face and can empathize with each other. This is the empathy and understanding which needs to be created world-wide amongst all peoples everywhere on Earth.

Once the world's people attain this understanding there is nothing to stop the Creation of a new and better world. The realization of solutions to the problems of war, greed, poverty, injustice, racism, environmental destruction, inequality and all the related issues that go along with them will come forth. Many solutions have already been given to humanity throughout history. It is simply choosing the best solution option at all times. There are now no problems on Earth but only solutions. Significant numbers of people on planet Earth have already developed solutions to problems the human race has experienced for too long now.

Never underestimate your abilities when it comes to being a factor in the changes which occur that improve the lives of humanity and all of the Creation. Simply praying for your fellow brothers and sisters on Earth has positive effects. All we can do is all we can do. Each one must decide for themselves what all they can do entails. Some will look at the practice of

7

meditation and consider it doing nothing. We are not one who has devoted a significant amount of time to the practice of meditation but according to personal accounts there are a number of positive benefits. Meditation could be looked at as a form of prayer and when done with good intent results in effects.

The makeup of this work as mentioned previously can be seen as divided into two parts. In Part One we will look at what we consider the most pressing issues of concern in the physical realm at this time. The issues are of fairly equal importance and magnitude. If we would have to rank the issues according to the amount of impact on humanity and all life the ranking could go as follows:

1. Genetically modified organisms, especially the patenting of plants/foods. The introduction of GMO foods poses a threat to human health which is unparalleled in human history. The magnitude of error to allow this untested science loose in the environment is unquantifiable. There are certain countries on Earth which have assessed the risks properly and labeled GMO food products or outright banned them. We will take a concise look at this issue touching upon major points for the reader's understanding of this most important problem. The God given right of human beings, along with all sentient beings, to food and water provided in abundance by Mother Earth is the goal.

2. Private central banking control of money. Given the current economic crises facing many countries on Earth the need for monetary reform is self apparent. National governments' historical need to borrow from private central banks as debt has resulted in strangulations of the economies and peoples of these countries. The time has come for the public, governmental control of monetary systems, the quantity of money, creation of money and credit to be realized by every nation on Earth. We will give you a historical look at banking which will give you a general knowledge of this enormously important issue. The ending of the negative historical consequences of greed suffered by humanity is the goal.

3. War. Given mankind's heartbreaking unacceptable negative consequences of wars every effort must be taken to end violence. Military force, when Spiritual and cooperative solutions are always available, should be used only in self defense. We will give detailed personal accounts from historical figures to allow the reader to feel the urgency of the need for ending wars. The causes of violent conflict will be covered to clear the errors of omission in the field of history. The establishment of Peace, justice and fairness on Earth is the goal.

4. Mainstream media. If, since the invention of the printed word, all media forms were used

to convey the true reality of events on Earth this work would be unnecessary. Unfortunately the honest, accurate reporting of important events through history in the media has not occurred. We will hear the words of those who were and are concerned about honest reporting of events in order to identify positive, creative new uses of the various media forms. Greater informing of the people as to the reality of what is actually happening on Earth is the goal.

The second part/Part Two of the work is devoted to the Spiritual realm. The answers/solutions to the major problems/issues faced by humanity in Part One are of Spirit. The writings will show the reader a Spiritual view of life that contributes to greater awareness of the possible application of the ideas/concepts toward problem solving for humanity. Spiritual wisdom is what is called for at all times in order for Love, Peace, justice, fairness, equality and compassion to spread over the Earth, her people and all life. The speedy balancing of human activity on Earth to a healthy Spirit/ego basis is the overall objective.

1. Gnostic writings. The gospel of Thomas and the Lost Book of John were two of many lost books/writings found in Nag Hammadi, Egypt in 1945. We have included extended excerpts from these two books as they have insights of a Spiritual nature which will give readers awareness beneficial to solving mankind's problems. The wisdom contained in the passages is of a kind that allows for those who read them more insight into the mysteries and meaning of life. When the events occurring in the physical realm are seen with Spiritual insight the chances are greatly improved that human actions taken will be correct and good. Decision making which will be the most beneficial for humanity and all of Creation is the goal.

2. A Course in Miracles. The work is a three-part self study course written between the years of 1965-1973. Compiled at the time by psychologist Dr. Helen Schucman from New York, the course is Spiritual psychotherapy. The writings are very profound and unlike other Spiritual works in levels of depth and intensity. A Course in Miracles reads like great poetry with what seems like every word being placed for maximum effect of instruction. Levels of Spiritual power come through the written words which transports the reader to a place of unparalleled insight and knowledge especially with regard to interpersonal relations. Developing an awareness of the profound, positive Spiritual potential of person to person interactions is the goal.

3. The near death experience. We give to the reader a number of personal descriptions given

by men and women who have had what has come to be termed the near death experience. The similarities between the personal accounts and experiences of these men, women and children are remarkable. Almost every experiencer describes a world of Spirit that is indescribable and beyond words. The words they use to try to describe the indescribable include visual scenery, auditory music and intense feelings which have profound effects on each person upon returning to their physical bodies. A high percentage go through a life review which when described give us valuable life lessons which can be applied to our lives along with the lives of all people on Earth. Increasing Spiritual knowledge of the possible meaning of life is the goal.

4. Selected quotes. Part Two concludes with a variety of thoughts and ideas in the form of quotations. The variety allows the reader to experience a number of contrasting examples of human thought. This exposure will contribute to the reader's synthesis of human thinking and an understanding of those characteristics which are common to all human beings. This synthesis will then contribute to the factors contained in a personal philosophy more inclined to actively become a base from which human Spiritual evolution is manifested. The ripple effect from person to person encompassing all mankind is the goal.

We now will share words spoken by Black Elk/Oglala Sioux warrior and medicine man. These are from the classic Spiritual book, "Black Elk Speaks" by John G. Neihardt.

Pointing at Harney Peak in the American Badlands where as a young man he received his great vision Black Elk, now an old man, speaks:

"There, when I was young, the Spirits took me in my vision to the center of the Earth and showed me all the good things in the Sacred hoop of the world. I wish I could stand up there in the flesh before I die, for there is something I want to say to the six grandfathers."

The trip to Harney Peak was arranged and on the way up Black Elk said to his son, Ben: "Something should happen today. If I have any power left, the thunder beings of the west should hear me when I send a voice, and there should be at least a little thunder and a little rain. Right over there is where I stood in my vision, but the hoop of the world about me was different, for what I saw was in Spirit."

Black Elk, standing in that same spot, holding the Sacred pipe before him in his right hand, spoke: "Hey-a-a-hey! Hey-a-a-hey! Hey-a-a-hey! Hey-a-a-hey! Grandfather, Great Spirit, once more behold me on Earth and lean to hear my feeble voice. You lived first, and you are older than all need, older than all prayer. All things belong to you-the two leggeds, the four leggeds, the wings of the air and all green things that live. You have set the powers of the four quarters to cross each other. The good road and the road of difficulties you have made to cross, the place is Holy. Day in and day out, forever, you are the life of things."

"Therefore I am sending a voice, Great Spirit, my grandfather, forgetting nothing you have made, the stars of the universe and the grasses of the Earth. You have said to me, when I was still young and could hope, that in difficulty I should send a voice four times, once for each quarter of the Earth, and you would hear me. Today I send a voice for a people in despair. You have given me a Sacred pipe, and through this I should make my offering. You see it now."

"From the west, you have given me the cup of living water and the Sacred bow, the power to make live and to destroy. You have given me a Sacred wind and the herb from where the white giant lives-the cleansing power and the healing. The daybreak star and the pipe, you have given from the east; and from the south, the nation's Sacred hoop and the tree that was to bloom. To the center of the world you have taken me and showed the goodness and the beauty and the strangeness of the greening Earth, the only Mother-and there the Spirit shapes of things, as they should be, you have shown to me and I have seen. At the center of this Sacred hoop you have said that I should make the tree to bloom."

"With tears running, o Great Spirit, Great Spirit, my grandfather-with running tears I must say now that the tree has never bloomed. A pitiful old man, you see me here, and I have fallen away and have done nothing. Here at the center of the world, where you took me when I was young and taught me; here, old, I stand, and the tree is withered, grandfather, my grandfather! Again, and maybe the last time on this Earth, I recall the great vision you sent me. It may be that some little root of the Sacred tree still lives. Nourish it then, that it may leaf and bloom and fill with singing birds. Hear me, not for myself, but for my people; I am old. Hear me that they may once more go back into the Sacred hoop and find the good red road, the shielding tree!"

"In sorrow I am sending a feeble voice, oh six powers of the world. Hear me in my sorrow, for I may never call again. Oh make my people live!"

For some minutes the old man stood silent, with face uplifted, weeping in the drizzling rain. In a little while the sky was clear.

Notes

Communication.

"We are born with a purpose in life and we have to fulfill that purpose. Some of our young men go out when they are twelve or thirteen years old and pray and fast at a certain Sacred place. They learn their purpose in life... Now we hear of the new young people talking about finding their identity, their place in life, and they are very wise to do that, if they can do it. Some of them have, I think, and they are trying to make things better for other people-which is our only purpose in life-to share with others." Rolling Thunder/Cherokee (1916-1997)

Rolling Thunder's words here came from the Native American Spiritual classic "Rolling Thunder" written by Doug Boyd in the mid-1970's. The sharing of his words at the beginning of this effort seemed right, as you and the writer will be going on an exploratory journey of discovery. We will be exploring various issues of major importance relating to our common experiences here in the physical realm. As the idea of all of us having a destiny and a purpose seems to be grasped more and more intensely while we move through time, it would seem that an examination of this fundamental idea should be undertaken. "What is God?", "What does life really mean?", "Why are we here?", "Why can't the people of the world create a society/living system on Earth where the problems like war, greed, poverty, starvation, environmental degradation, etc. are solved once and for all?". What are the solutions?

If you were fortunate enough to have read the book "Rolling Thunder" by Doug Boyd, perhaps you resonated with the Spiritual concepts and ideas shared by Rolling Thunder. Given the contents of that particular work, there is no doubt that you were profoundly moved upon absorbing the honest articulation shared graciously by Rolling Thunder with the help of Doug Boyd. Searchers of truth are appreciative whenever they discover works which contain honest writing and articulation.

Throughout human history men and women have shared their ideas and thoughts with regard to the perennial condition. Generation after generation of our ancestors were dealing with the same issues and problems that we are still trying to resolve up to now. Is it possible to finally, create a world where the age-old problems are solved once and for all? The answer is a resounding "Yes!" The solutions are Spiritual.

Mohandes Gandhi (1869-assassinated 1948).

"Ahimsa [infinite Love} is a weapon of matchless potency. It is the summum bonum. (n. The greatest or supreme good of life) It is an attribute of the brave, in fact it is their all. It does not come within reach of the coward. It is no wooden or lifeless dogma but a living and life-giving force. It is the special attribute of the soul." (Spoken: May 29, 1924).

Gandhi, along with many other men and women throughout human history, had come to a certain point in their respective experiences where the concept of "Infinite Love" had been understood to be a real, tangible one for them. This can be nothing less than proof positive that the Creation of a world where our problems are solved is entirely possible. Can we imagine, like John Lennon, "...All the people, sharing all the world."? John Lennon along with many others were and are talking about a very real possibility. Anything that man can imagine he can create. We have all felt the sadness and compassion when observing the news reports showing our fellow human brothers and sisters suffering every kind of pain up to death. Does it not seem that this has become an untenable (adj. Being such that defense or maintenance is impossible) situation?

How long will we continue to place these absolutely searing images out of mind, out of sight as we watch our American Idol, our sports programs, our fictional situation comedies, our fictional dramas and our "reality shows" on our 80" plasma televisions? What will it take to bring us to a point where those who are concerned about solving these immense life problems are no longer in the minority, mostly unseen by the majority of the human population on the mass media? When will these men and women be given their chance to share possible solutions on the 80" plasma?

The television is the major form of mass communication for the human race. We simply must ask ourselves what has been going on since the invention of television that has resulted in programming that, for what seems to be 99% of the total air time, has virtually nothing in it that pertains to the human issues and problems of our times. What has been going on?

Perhaps we need only to read the words at the end of journalism Professor Ben Bagdikian's book "The Media Monopoly", written in 1983, where he says, "If this generation of Americans exercises its responsibilities to political morality, it will be following the dictates of eighty years ago by that remarkable physician-philosopher William James: 'The deadliest enemies of nations... Always dwell within their borders. And from these internal enemies civilization is always in need of being saved. The nation blest above all is she in whom the civic genius of the people does the saving day by day, by acts without external picturesqueness; by speaking, writing, voting reasonably; by smiting corruption swiftly; by good temper between parties; by the people knowing true men when they see them, and preferring them as leaders

14

to rabid partisans or empty quacks.' ".

Mr. Bagdikian's 1983 book deals with the media ownership situation at that time where the media was becoming more and more owned by fewer corporations. Men and women sit on the boards of media conglomerates as well as on the boards of oil, banking and manufacturing corporations to the point where we can easily see why there are no investigative reports of certain organizations seeing the light of day on your 80" plasma. This phenomena is called "interlocking directorates" and is summed up by Mr. Bagdikian when he says: "...which way will the common oil/RCA (RCA owned NBC at the time) director vote 'in the best interests of' conflicting corporations?"

Louis Brandeis, before joining the Supreme Court, wrote: "The practice of interlocking directorates is the root of many evils. It offends laws human and divine... It tends to disloyalty and violation of the fundamental law that no man can serve two masters... It is undemocratic, for it rejects the platform: 'a fair field and no favors.' ".

Basically "The Media Monopoly" points out that the reality of interlocking directorates results in a form of media censorship. Any news of relevance concerning large corporations which is of a negative nature will probably not be seen, read or heard of by the average television viewer and reader. Unfortunately the consolidation of the media into fewer and fewer owners/conglomerates has only accelerated since 1983. Hence the information we receive from sources other than alternative media or the internet has been, in all probability, been sanitized.

Did you ever notice that the night-time programs such as "20/20", "Primetime", "Nightline" etc. seem to always deal with stories involving one family or other stories where the content pertains to only a handful of people? This, it would seem, gives proof that the sanitization of "news" is a reality. Can you imagine what progress we as humans could have been making during all these passing years if air time was devoted to the most important issues and problems facing us all? Such a potentially powerful tool which has been so drastically under utilized.

Bruce Springsteen wrote the song "57 Channels (And Nothing On)" years ago which sums up his agreement with the awareness that television programming choices have been an example of the wasted opportunities to utilize the power of communication inherent in the television media. So much potential. So much wisdom, especially from the world's elders, could be being shared with everyone on Earth. Think about all the real wisdom that is available from our elders to be shared right now. Wouldn't you be interested if there was a channel on your cable listing devoted to those who were concerned with solving major human problems?

Would not this wisdom be of so much more value to us than the words of teenagers from the entertainment industry or the words of professional athletes or the words of power hungry, greedy politicians? Does it not seem that the wisdom of the grandmothers and grandfathers gives us a much greater chance of arriving at truth? Our elders are to be respected above all according to many Spiritual traditions, including those who some call "primitive". To you who read these words, please remember. Do give the utmost respect to the elders. It is a law. Please give respect to all livings things. The principle of not harming others is the number one principle of all. This includes all people, all life and all things. But the elders, especially, absolutely must be respected.

Let us get to the heart of the press/media issue with the help of some historical quotes. We are partial to the use of quotes as they are the gems of individuals' wisdom and summarize the most important thoughts the person has come to in their human experience. The words and thoughts contained in these quotes were worthy of recording and sharing.

Speaking about the press American historian Henry (Brooks) Adams (1838-1918) said in 1862: "The press is the hired agent of a moneyed system, and set up for no other purpose than to tell lies where their interests are involved. One can trust nobody and nothing." Ponder the next time you click on the "news".

English reformer Charles Bradlaugh (1833-1891) said in 1890: "Without free speech no search for truth is possible... No discovery of truth is useful... Better a thousand-fold abuse of free speech than denial of free speech. The abuse dies in a day, but the denial slays the life of the people, and entombs the hope of the race."

Have you ever wondered why there are not any channels for world leaders to express their thoughts on the most pressing concerns of the day? Would it not be very useful if men and women around the planet could tune in to those channels and gain a better understanding of the true situations on the ground where there have been warnings of potential military conflict? Or where there exists a humanitarian crisis as a result of natural disaster or wars? The technology is available for world-wide broadcasting of solutions based information. What are we waiting for?

American writer Theodore Dreiser (1871-1945) said in 1942: "The American press, with a very few exceptions, is a kept press. Kept by the big corporations the way a whore is kept by a rich man." We apologize, for some of the information we are sharing with you is not the most positive. We simply believe that the awareness of these realities is necessary for people to have so that truth will be able to emerge. Truth must and will emerge in the very near future as we, the human race, are going to experience, and are experiencing now, a raising of consciousness which will be simply unstoppable. Many are aware of these changes coming from the Creator at this time and are glad. These changes will result in the human race becoming aware of their divine origins. There is nothing anyone can do to stop this. This will be the ultimate event in human history as our Spiritual/physical balance will be restored. We will all come to understand infinite, unconditional Love.

U.S. Supreme Court Justice William O. Douglas (1898-1980) in his dissent, Earl Caldwell case of 1972, said: "The function of the press is to explore and investigate events, inform the people what is going on, and to expose the harmful as well as the good influences at work. There is no higher function performed under our constitutional regime... A reporter is no better than his source of information. Unless he has a privilege to withhold the identity of his source, he will be the victim of governmental intrigue or aggression. If he can be summoned to testify in secret before a grand jury, his sources will dry up and the attempted exposure, the effort to enlighten the public will be ended..."

"...The intrusion of government into this domain is symptomatic of the disease of this society. As the years pass, the power of government becomes more and more pervasive. It is power to suffocate both people and causes. Those in power, whatever their politics, want only to perpetuate it. Now that the fences of the law and the tradition that has protected the press are broken down, the people are the victims. The first amendment, as I read it, was designed precisely to prevent that tragedy."

Justice Douglas was one who thought the maturity of a nation was reflected in its acceptance of a dissident press. Perhaps most folks think a dissident press is one that expresses differing opinions than the mainstream press. Perhaps the time slots taken by one of the "reality" shows could be devoted to debates between the mainstream and dissident presses.

One of America's great men, third President Thomas Jefferson (1743-1826) had this to say about newspapers: "Nothing can now be believed which is seen in a newspaper. Truth itself becomes suspicious by being put in that polluted vehicle." Jefferson also said: "Perhaps an editor might begin a reformation in some such way as this. Divide his paper into four chapters. Heading the 1st: truths, 2nd: probabilities, 3rd: possibilities, 4th: lies. The first chapter would be very short."

This was during a time when newspapers were the only media. It is unfortunate that the absence of truths that Jefferson mentioned has persisted until now. Thank the Creator for that powerful communication tool that we call the internet. The ability of men and women to talk and share ideas with anyone on Earth. We should all be expressing gratitude for this Godsend. The positive results of all the on-going chats and the sharing of ideas across national borders have surely been only blessings. With the continuing improvements in communication technologies we can only be more and more grateful. Can you feel the joy experienced by all the men and women who have really connected in a good way with this most blessed tool? Can you see how this internet is a divine tool which has contributed mightily to the powerful changes which we are literally seeing occur before our very eyes? The internet allows all of humanity to keep the faith.

American newspaper publisher Joseph Pulitzer (1847-1911) said on his retirement: "...Always fight for progress and reform, never tolerate injustice and corruption, always fight demagogues of all parties, never belong to any party, always oppose privileged classes and public plunderers, never lack sympathy with the poor, always remain devoted to the public welfare, never be satisfied with merely printing news; always be drastically independent; never be afraid to attack wrong, whether by predatory plutocracy or predatory poverty." We can see why the Pulitzer Prize was named in his honor. Pray that more journalists and writers come to accept the thoughts that Joseph Pulitzer shared with us.

American press lord E.W. Scripps (1854-1926) said: "The press of this country is now and always has been so thoroughly dominated by the wealthy few of the country, that it cannot be depended upon to give the great mass of the people that correct information concerning political, economical, and social subjects which it is necessary that the mass of people shall have, in order that they shall vote and in all ways act in the best way to protect themselves from the brutal force and the chicanery of the ruling class."

Once again, thank God for the internet. By now you are getting some idea of the realities of the media/press that are not well known. This awareness is vital to you because once this awareness is achieved you will no longer see, hear or watch mass media in the same ways that you did before. You will no longer pass along information you received from the media to others as if it was the gospel truth. Then the spread of untruths and propaganda from the mainstream media will diminish as men and women find truthful information elsewhere.

Imagine how much time and energy is wasted in conversations and communications where the ideas shared are based on false information or outright lies.

Everyone has experienced talking with others and being astonished with the errors conveyed. Sometimes we are astonished because others have thankfully corrected us. Please remember to be as honest and open-minded that you can be in all of your communications. This will guarantee the greatest possibility for the real exchange of ideas and the understandings that we need to share.

Editor of the New York Sun John Swinton (1830-1901) said in 1893: "There is no such thing as an independent press in America. I am paid to keep my honest opinions out of the paper I am connected with. Any of you who would be so foolish as to write honest opinions would be out on the street looking for another job. We are the tools and vassals of the rich men behind the scenes. We are the jumping jacks; they pull the strings and we dance. Our talents, our possibilities and our lives are all the property of other men. We are intellectual prostitutes."

Seems that Mr. Swinton had come to a point where he had no fear of retribution. The honesty of his words here is something to behold. The willingness to share his thoughts in this way gives us hope and faith that journalists and reporters will give us the reality of events. What a sad situation it must be to belong to a group called intellectual prostitutes. It is understandable that those who have gone to university to study journalism, broadcasting and related fields have a really tough time with regard to the decisions that need to be made concerning employment.

We have compassion for these men and women. Thank our Creator/Source/God that they along with all of us, very soon, will be relieved of these moral choices we have to make as the answers will become obvious to us. The possibility of choosing the immoral will be no longer available. The moral choice will be the only choice.

Returning to our examination of the media/press we have a quote from American social scientist Thorstein Veblen (1857-1929): "The first duty of an editor is to gauge the sentiment of the reader, and then to tell them what they like to believe... His second duty is to see that nothing is said in the news items or editorials which may discountenance any claims or announcements made by the advertisers, discredit their standing or good faith, or expose many weaknesses or deception in any business venture that is or may become a valuable advertiser."

The words/thoughts expressed on the media here are very enlightening. Thankfully there are other sources besides those which depend on advertising revenue. Perhaps books would be a good alternative. There are many websites where one can go to read on-line books. There are books on CD that one can listen to while in the car. Personally we like to read books the old fashioned way... an actual book. At any rate we are getting the feel for what the media/press is all about. Pray for those who are employed at the various forms of organizations involved with the media communications industry who would love to be able to spend their time and energy pursuing their profession more in line with the thoughts expressed in quotes here.

Wish them all Godspeed and forgive them because you understand now the constraints they are dealing with. These men and women have families, mortgages, credit cards, utilities and all the rest that we are all dealing with. For that matter, forgive everyone for everything, realizing that the spark of the Holy Spirit and God is in all of us without exception. This Spiritual power is not only in us, the two-legged. It is in the four-legged, the winged, the crawling things, the green things, the air, the water, those that live in the water, the Mother Earth... All of Creation.

In your prayers please include all these as this will help more than you know. The prayers we make, no matter the form they take when expressed honestly, are heard in the Spiritual place which is our home. Our eternal home. Never for an instant fail to believe that your prayers and honest thoughts regarding the improvement of all life on our planet Earth are heard. Believe that these improvements are already on their way and that we will all soon be experiencing Love, joy and Peace in here-to-fore unseen ways that are unprecedented in human history.

What could the ideal media forms look like? What evidence would show that the human race is growing in the area of mass communication? We left a phone message with an un-named United States Senator a while back suggesting a world-wide satellite broadcast giving the leader of every nation on Earth say, 15-30 minutes to express to the people on the planet their thoughts on realistic solutions for the most pressing problems we face. This project's programming would be aired on prime-time television around the globe.

The leaders could videotape their segment and it would be a simple project requiring nothing special with regard to production. The feeling behind the event would be one where the participants would be aware of the reason for it is healing the Creation. Say, that wouldn't be a bad title for the event. "The Healing of the Creation." Win-Win. This was simply an idea that came across that seemed to make common sense. After leaving the message years ago we have seen nothing anywhere regarding this possibility.

We can imagine the response of those with the power to actualize this idea would go something like this: "Well, it sounds like a good idea, but we're afraid no-one would be interested. Nobody would watch." To that sentiment we would say: "Are you for real?" There is an old saying "There is such a thing as a free press, if you own one." In our view an event like this would be ground-breaking, record-shattering journalism that would be watched by more people than watch the Oscars and the Super Bowl combined. This type of idea, if actualized, would transform life on this planet.

It was simply an idea which came up randomly as our thoughts often do. We would be willing to bet that you readers have all had these types of "random" thoughts come to you. The "random" thoughts that, when you become aware of them, have you ask yourself: "Maybe this is an idea that could work. I should bring this up with someone who can make it happen." Perhaps you take action. Perhaps you don't. Perhaps, seeing the airwaves are owned by the people, the people should have a much larger say in how those airwaves are utilized.

Imagine all of the positive programming that could be made available to the people of the Earth. Imagine all of the problems that will be solved, what a much better world we will be leaving to our children and grandchildren and great-grandchildren. Let us pray to the Great Spirit for this dream of utilizing these excellent communication tools for the literal improvement of the human condition become a reality now.

Imagine a world where the idea of seven generations is understood by all. This is the philosophy of the Native Americans where every action one takes is taken with the concern in mind of how that action will affect those unborn until seven generations from now. Would this not result in an actual Heaven on Earth? The possibilities are endless and the time is now.

Another area where media reform would be useful is in the area of political campaigning. The problems associated with fund-raising for political runs for office seem to be in need of some type of resolution. How can we go along with the current state of affairs where those candidates who raise the most money have the advantage over their opponents who raise less? The recent Supreme Court ruling in Citizens United v. Federal Election Commission allowing unlimited spending on political campaigns by corporations and unions, our common sense would tell us, was simply a wrong decision. Since then super-pacs have spent twice as much money on television advertising than the candidates' campaigns.

Candidates are prohibited from having any contact with super-pacs, but, come on. Anytime there are large amounts of money involved you can bet there will be corruption. Power and money are such huge drivers of those involved in politics that Citizens United v. Federal Election Commission will be overturned. The fox guarding the henhouse would be the correct comparison here for obvious reasons. Montana has had a campaign finance case with connection to Citizens United and has led to two U.S. Supreme Court justices suggesting reconsideration. Ruth Bader Ginsburg and Stephen G. Breyer have come out with doubts about the decision and the course of events since the ruling.

We have seen the unlimited spending begin and will only go to the stratosphere if the decision is not overturned and soon. Given that a number of States have taken steps to have the decision overturned would allow us to predict that the decision will, in fact, be overturned. Any arguments for or against the decision will, when compared, come down decidedly for overturn. The sentiments of the American people will lead to the overturn simply because it lacks fairness.

One has to feel for the media corporations as their revenues from political advertising would have been guaranteed at a high level were it not for the overturn of the decision. But then, one should rejoice because one will not be subjected to an endless barrage of commercials where candidates and super-pacs attack their opponents with the latest untruths.

One thing we can say with regard to the Citizens United case is that it has turned out to be such a huge decision that the average citizen has gained an awareness of the problems associated with campaign spending. The increased awareness of the people will be the spark that starts the fire which will result in far reaching, comprehensive campaign finance reform. The final product will totally ban money from the political process. No candidate for any office in the United States of America will have, as a condition for running, raising money at the top of his or her list.

Political advertising of any kind will be prohibited. The only way a candidate will be allowed to "advertise" will be with their ideas and thoughts given during debates on television or radio. Air time will be given freely for debates by television and radio stations. Perhaps some form of public financing of elections would be needed, but what is wrong with the public gaining their knowledge of candidate views only through the broadcasted debates? It would seem that the probability of the election of the most qualified candidates would be increased. The people would decide who to support based on ideas only. This would be, when simply looking at the suggestion, the ideal way to determine elections... Perfect. Another benefit of choosing this form of elections would be that, after the successful candidate has proven to the people that his or her ideas are preferable and is elected to office, he or she can devote all of their time dealing with all of the important issues of the day, instead of raising money for the next election.

No longer will there be any need for he or she to spend any time raising money for the next election. People have come to have a low opinion of our political leaders because of the influence of money. Taking money out of the political process would begin the process of building real democracy as more time would devoted to addressing and solving problems facing the human race. How blind must we be to hold on to a system where those with the financial power have the advantage simply because they can outspend their opponents on advertising and do not have to rely on the real source of leadership which is ideas. What are we waiting for?

Before the Presidential election of 2000 between Gore and Bush we wrote a letter to the editor about Presidential debates. The letter was published in the "letters to the editor" section of a major newspaper in Chicago, Illinois. Our suggestion was for a series of five debates, not only between Gore and Bush but including all candidates from recognized parties, which would be nationally televised during prime-time with a length of three hours each. The debates would deal with the important topics such as war and Peace, economics, public health, the Earth's environment and personal philosophy/Spirituality.

How can it be that we accept the current Presidential debate format where only two candidates debate three times at maybe 60 minutes each? Many regard the office as the most powerful on Earth and we give so little time to the people for their decision making? Would it be a cruel thing to subject the candidates to having to actually expound on their ideas in detail? The election of a President happens only once every four years. Should not we be devoting substantial time for the people to study the candidates' ideas and weigh them so they can ideally make the best choice? College professors, high school teachers, experts in all fields of endeavor expound for hundreds of hours during their courses on all manner of specific areas of study.

Surely Presidential candidates have the ability to express in detail their ideas and views for much longer debate periods. If candidates cannot fill the hours they are given to answer with detail their ideas to the American people, then the American people will make their voting decisions accordingly. Once again, this would lead to a higher percentage of candidates being elected where the people made actual, reasoned choices when they stepped into the voting booth. Is this not the better way to go, where democracy becomes more real?

So we have taken a look at the internet, television, radio, newspapers from a historical perspective. It seems that the conditions have not changed much through the centuries. We have cause for hope with the rise of the world-wide-web, where people have the tremendous ability to reach out to each other and share viewpoints and philosophies. We can safely express our gratitude for this gift which has become an engine for the building of real democracy around the world.

It has become very difficult for those who wish to keep secrets from our brothers and sisters to retain that ability. This is good. If one has come to the conclusion that there are no differences amongst us, that we are all the same children of God, then there are no longer any reasons for secrecy. Now we witness the ever increasing grasp of the events that have been kept in secret coming to light. With this ever increasing awareness we will be willing to speak out whenever we see corruption, greed, unnecessary violence and suffering... All those human activities which should make us feel regret, sadness and a determination to fix.

The musical group Coldplay has a song titled "Fix You". One line of the lyrics reads: "...Lights will guide you home, and ignite your bones and I will try to fix you..." Perhaps, after all, this is one of the main, if not the main reason we are alive in the human skin. To fix each other. To heal each other through the mutual awareness that we are all one. We are all the same. When Jesus said: "Whatever you do to the least of these, you do to me." he was pointing out a universal law. We are all one. It is all one. Everything that we see, touch and feel is Sacred. If one reaches the point where Sacredness is seen in everything then it would be impossible to harm anything. If everyone came to the same realization there would be a total elimination of harm. Would this not seem to be a worthy goal?

Forgive them father they know not what they do. Let us forgive them all as they have not known what they have done. Spiritual power is returning to us here on Mother Earth. Commensurate with this Spiritual power is equal return of wisdom.

French writer and existentialist Jean-Paul Sartre (1905-1980) said: "If you begin by saying, 'thou shalt not lie', there is no longer any possibility of political action." This is why it is so important to base the election of political leaders on what they convey during lengthy debates. There must be a minimization of the chance that candidates who are less than totally honest will be elected. Lengthy debates, available for all to see and hear, will result in the maximization of the chance that totally honest candidates will be elected.

French Statesman Alexis de Tocqueville (1805-1859) said: "I know of no country in which there is so little true independence of mind and freedom of discussion as in America... The majority raises very formidable barriers to the liberty of opinion; within these barriers an author may write whatever he pleases, but he will repent it if he ever steps beyond them. Not that he is exposed to the terrors of an auto-da-fe (public execution during the inquisition), but he is tormented by the slights and persecutions of daily obloquy (censure, blame or abusive language aimed at a person). His political career is closed forever." As few as one can speak the truth. The major social changes which have occurred throughout our human history were begun with an idea, many times by one man or woman speaking their truth.

British novelist and historian H.G. Wells (1866-1946) had an interesting take on politics. He said: "My idea of politics is an open conspiracy to hurry these tiresome, wasteful, evil things-- nationality and war-- out of existence; to end this empire and that empire, and set up one empire of man."

One must appreciate Wells' directness. Seems like thought very worthy of emulation. He was spot-on with his description of nationality and war being "tiresome, wasteful, evil things." You probably feel the same way as we do. Let's hurry these tiresome, wasteful, evil things out of existence. It is the year 2012. Now is the time.

War.

War. Mankind's greatest failure. How many of you have had enough of war? Great Spirit answer our prayers. Please help us finally put an end to this error of war that we keep repeating and repeating. Please put an end to the causes of fighting amongst our fellow human beings with its massive suffering inflicted on both "winners" and "losers" alike. For there is no "winning" in war, only loss.

Here we would offer the words of the 34th President of the United States, Dwight Eisenhower (1890-1969): "Every gun that is made, every warship launched, every rocket fired, signifies in the final sense a theft from those who hunger and are not fed, those who are cold and are not clothed. This world in arms is not spending money alone. It is spending the sweat of its laborers, the genius of its scientists, the houses of its children. This is not a way of life... Under the cloud of war, it is humanity hanging itself on a cross of iron."

You would think that such a frank analysis as this one made by Eisenhower with its profundity would have turned the tide concerning war and military expenditure. Eisenhower, in his farewell address, adds yet another profound look at the military expenditures of mankind: "This conjunction of an immense military establishment and a large arms industry is new in the American experience... In the councils of government, we must guard against the acquisition of unwarranted influence, whether sought or unsought, by the military-industrial complex. The potential for the disastrous rise of misplaced power exists and will persist."

Why do we end up disregarding the obvious wisdom through history men and women have given us? Eisenhower's words in these two quotes are simply spot-on. What a predicament we have put ourselves in with regard to military spending and the use of the products created with that spending. Thank God we are coming to the point in time where our Spiritual wisdom will be returned to us all. Finally, we will end this war madness once and for all. Divine intervention will make us all painfully aware of the error of our ways when we made the choices to allow this insanity to occur. You may want to read Eisenhower's words again and again until you really understand what he was trying to convey.

We have had war for so long now that it seems almost to be a part of life. It need not be so. War is a choice. If there was a reason for war it could only be self-defense. Any war of aggression must result in consequences which are severe enough for those responsible for their decisions to deter any future decision maker from making the same mistake. War crimes are the highest of any crimes and must be dealt with in the highest way. Many of you are aware that wars, most of the time, are fought for financial or natural resource reasons.

You may have read the book "Confessions of an Economic Hit-man" by John Perkins. The book was Perkins' insider view of geopolitical events he participated in and witnessed. Mr. Perkins wrote the book after the September 11, 2001 World Trade Center event in an effort to create a better world for his children and grandchildren. He describes the typical course of events when he was dealing with the leaders of countries which had natural resources that multi-national companies wanted to have access to.

First, the leader and his country are given loans from the World Bank or the International Monetary Fund for large infrastructure projects which benefit mainly multi-national companies along with the elite of the country. The poor of the country do not realize any gain in their standard of living. Next the country falls behind on the repayment of the loans, in the billions of dollars. At this point Perkins describes the "pound of flesh". He would offer that particular country's leader great wealth if he played the game and allowed access at a low price to his country's natural resources. Of course, austerity measures would be needed in order that the World Bank/IMF loans could be repaid.

He would gently remind the leader, if he was considering not playing the game, of what happened to the previous leader who did not want to play. It is called political assassination. Perkins dealt personally with democratically elected leaders who were killed in airplane crashes etc. If the current leader continues to reject the offers then the jackals are sent in to attempt a coup or political dissent; any action that would drive the leader from office, including assassination. Then, if this fails to remove the leader, the military comes to forcibly remove the leader through war. What Perkins describes is very saddening.

Thanks to John Perkins for telling the world the truth through his experiences on the geopolitical stage. The book is an eye opener for whoever reads it and, even though the book describes a very sad state of affairs, has contributed to a needed awareness of the reality of what he describes being gained for people from many areas of the planet. This awareness has served as a defense for many against such manipulative actions with the unfortunate consequences associated with them. People have been spared suffering and hardship because John Perkins stood up and told the truth.

Many other books have been written by men and women who have experienced war. As wars are started by the rich and fought by the poor we will be giving no voice here to those who start wars. Only if those who started the war risked their own lives and safety will they receive any mention. We have all seen those who received deferments or somehow escaped danger themselves calling for others to fight for them. We will concentrate on those men and women who actually have experienced the horrors of war. Their stories and their thoughts.

Perhaps you may have heard of marine Major General Smedley Butler (1881-1940). He wrote a book with the title "War is a Racket". Read these harrowing words: "I spent 33 years and four months in active military service and during that period I spent most of my time as a high class muscleman for big business, for Wall Street and the bankers. In short I was a racketeer, a gangster for capitalism. I helped make Mexico and especially Tampico safe for American oil interests in 1914. I helped make Haiti and Cuba a decent place for the National City Bank boys to collect revenues in. I helped in the raping of half a dozen Central American republics for the benefit of Wall Street. I helped purify Nicaragua for the international banking house of Brown Brothers in 1902-1912. I brought light to the

Dominican Republic for the American sugar interests in 1916. I helped make Honduras right for the American Fruit companies in 1903. In China in 1927 I helped see to it that Standard Oil went on its way unmolested. Looking back on it, I might have given Al Capone a few hints. The best he could do was to operate his racket in three districts. I operated in three continents."

Do you ever wonder why we are experiencing the Spiritual pain associated with wars and violence? Sometimes you just want to yell out, God please end this war insanity. Help us to end war and create the conditions for everlasting Love, Justice and Peace on Earth. Please pray.

The words of Native American Chief Joseph, upon surrender, contain the real testimony from the heart of a human regarding the effects of conflict. Feel the same feeling that Chief Joseph conveys in these words and you will never see war in the same way again.

He said: "Tell General Howard I know his heart. What he told me before, I have in my heart. I am tired of fighting. Our chiefs are killed, Looking-Glass is dead, Too-Hul-Hul Sote is dead. The old men are all dead. It is the young men who say yes or no. He who led on the young men is dead. It is cold, and we have no blankets; the little children are freezing to death. My people, some of them, have run away to the hills, and have no blankets, no food. No one knows where they are-perhaps freezing to death. I want to have time to look for my children, and see how many of them I can find. Maybe I shall find them among the dead. Hear me, my chiefs! I am tired; my heart is sick and sad. From where the sun now stands, I will fight no more forever."

The emotional state Chief Joseph was in when he spoke these words is the same emotional state that every human experiences after war. We now understand what causes post traumatic stress syndrome. It is the direct result of the horrifying experiences that these brothers and sisters have when involved in military conflict. With the understanding of the suffering that our fellow humans experience because of war we must ask ourselves... What type of insanity calls for more suffering? War is insanity.

American writer Samuel Clemens ("Mark Twain") (1835-1910) wrote the "War Prayer" in 1904. It would seem that he came to a point where, grappling with issues of war and Peace, the concepts required so much effort in his mind that he wrote the "War Prayer" out of utter frustration. Twain wrote: "O lord our father, our young patriots, idols of our hearts, go forth to battle-be thou near them! ...O lord our God, help us to tear their soldiers to bloody shreds with our shells; help us to cover their smiling fields with the pale forms of their patriot dead: help us to drown the thunder of the guns with the shrieks of their wounded, writhing in pain; help us to lay waste their humble homes with the hurricane of fire; help us to wring the hearts of their unoffending widows with unavailing grief... For our sakes who adore thee, lord, blast their hopes, blight their lives, protract their bitter pilgrimage, make heavy their steps, water their way with their tears, stain the white snow with the blood of their wounded feet! We ask it in the Spirit of Love, of him who is the source of Love, and who is the ever-faithful refuge and friend of all who are sore beset and seek his aid with humble and contrite hearts. Amen."

Samuel Clemens was a genius; one who possessed extraordinary intellectual and creative power. Read the "War Prayer" again and you will sense what Clemens was feeling when he wrote it.

American writer and editor Norman Cousins (1915-1990) said: "War is an invention of the human mind. The human mind can invent Peace." Does it not give one hope for the future when one sees the thoughts of our fellow human brothers and sisters which point to such intelligence? As we mentioned elsewhere we are partial to quotations as they allow us to share the thoughts of genius personalities, past and present, without the requirement of actually being in their physical presence. How simple yet profound Norman Cousins' words are here. The human mind can invent Peace. Simple. Profound.

Our faith in the certain triumph of the human Spirit is restored when we come across such intellectual depth and insight. English poet and critic John Dryden (1631-1700) stated a basic truth about the cause of war: "War seldom enters but where wealth allures."

Does not this thought equal that expressed in 1 Timothy 6:10: "For the love of money is the root of all evil." The love of money... How much longer will some love money more than their fellow human family? Love it so much that they are willing to kill others in order to acquire it? Love it so much that they willing to destroy everything in their way to get to it? Love it so much that they are willing to sell their own souls to obtain it? The artists have been asking these questions for a very long time. With the current, fortunate raising of consciousness on planet Earth, thank the Creator that these questions will not have to be asked anymore soon. We, the human race, are going to get all of our questions answered. It is our destiny.

German born, Swiss-American scientist Albert Einstein (1879-1955) said the following to Dr. Freud in 1932: "This is the problem: Is there any way of delivering mankind from the menace of war? ...As one immune from national bias, I personally see a simple way of dealing with the superficial (i.e. administrative) aspect of the problem: the setting up by international consent of a legislative and judicial body to settle every conflict arising between nations... Thus I am led to my first axiom: the quest of international security involves the unconditional surrender by every nation, in a certain measure, of its liberty of action, its sovereignty that is to say, and it is clear beyond doubt that no other road can lead to such security."

Einstein's last written words before he passed away showed how concerned he was about the solving of the problems facing humanity: "Not one Statesman in a position of responsibility has dared to pursue the only course that holds out any promise of Peace, the courage of supra-national security, since for a Statesman to follow such a course would be tantamount to political suicide."

Why is it that these words from the genius Einstein are rarely if ever diseminated, spread out far and wide. The reason is probably just as Einstein said: "...political suicide." We have decided to write down Einstein's thoughts here because they are important thoughts that the people should be aware of. They are more important than political suicide. Wisdom should not and will not be withheld for any reasons. The dissemination of wisdom results in solutions being implemented.

War goes back a very long way. Chinese philosopher and founder of Taoism Lao-Tzu (c.565 B.C.): "In time of war men, civilized in Peace, turn from their higher to their lower nature. But triumph is not beautiful. One who thinks triumph is beautiful is one with a will to kill. The death of a multitude is cause for mourning. Conduct your triumph as a funeral." And Lao-Tzu also said, "To rejoice in conquest is to rejoice in murder."

Humanity is coming to a point where we will truly understand the errors of our actions. We have yet to fully grasp the Spiritual aspects of all of our actions, both on a personal and on a global level. Thankfully the awareness that we have yet to fully grasp is inevitable. Human error, including error on the personal level involving all those we come into contact with, as well as nation to nation contacts, is being revealed. These historical errors will be resolved along with the damage done to both the individual and collective. From that point, because the human race has come to understand the error of its way, error will be no more. Then the human race will rejoice not in conquest, but in Peace. Then the human race will rejoice not in murder, but in healing.

American General Douglas MacArthur (1880-1964) is a well known historical military figure. MacArthur had some not so well known things to say about war that we could study: "I know war as few other men now living know it, and nothing to me is more revolting. I have long advocated its complete abolition, as its very destructiveness on both friend and foe has rendered it useless as a method of settling international disputes."

MacArthur spoke these words to Congress in 1951 when he was 71 years old. We have heard the famous quote from him "Old soldiers never die; they just fade away." but the quote where he pointed to "War rendered useless" seems to show us an instance where there is a selective use of MacArthur's thoughts and words. Are you aware of MacArthur speaking the following words in 1961 when he was 81 years old? "Global war has become a

Frankenstein's monster, threatening to destroy both sides... It contains now only the germs of a double suicide."

We are, if we have never experienced war on the personal level, getting some idea of the actual toll taken on mankind. MacArthur in the winter of his life came to the point where he had to try to prevent future generations from having to pay the same tolls with their horrifying consequences.

English dramatist Christopher Marlowe (1564-1593): "Accurst be he that first invented war." Marlowe spoke those words in the year 1587.

Lord chancellor of England, canonized 1915, Sir Thomas More (1478-beheaded 1535) wrote a book with the title "Utopia" in 1516. His words about an ideal society from the book, about war: "They detest war as a very brutal thing; and which, to the reproach of human nature is more practiced by men than any sort of beasts; and they, against the custom of almost all other nations, think that there is nothing more inglorious than that glory which is gained by war. They should be both troubled and ashamed of a bloody victory over their enemies; and in no victory do they glory so much, as in that which is gained by dexterity and good conduct without bloodshed."

Sir Thomas More is telling us that glory is a misunderstood word with regard to human relations. We could take this idea down to the personal level. We would feel a great honor when we chose dexterity and good conduct to resolve personal differences over the dishonorable choice of using anger or physical violence. Imagine all the suffering which could have been avoided throughout history if humanity would have chosen the real glory, with dexterity and good conduct, in situations where war and Peace was concerned. We have been given the wisdom all through human history to make the best choices.

All that is needed is the will to always have those best choices on the table. If we can always compare the alternatives does it not seem the best choices are going to be made? One need not have a doctoral degree in international relations to understand the simple, yet profound. These writings are not for those who have advanced degrees; it hopefully will not delve into minutiae but main points only. None of us have the time to waste on small, trivial details. We could give you minutiae but we will not. This work is for all people no matter their status.

Swedish munitions manufacturer and philanthropist Alfred Nobel (1833-1896) initiating the Nobel Prize: "I intend to leave after my death a large fund for the promotion of the Peace idea, but I am skeptical as to its results. The savants will write excellent volumes. There will be laureates. But wars will continue just the same until the force of circumstances renders them impossible."

We would submit that the force of circumstances has been present all along. They have not been taken into consideration, they have been ignored. The circumstance of human suffering, the circumstance of greed, the circumstance of wealth concentration, the circumstance of starvation, the circumstance of poverty, the circumstance of disease, the circumstance of environmental degradation, the circumstance of corruption, the circumstance of Spiritual bankruptcy.

The circumstance of believing the false notion that "We cannot create a Heaven on Earth." The circumstance of failing to heed Dwight Eisenhower's warning in his farewell address, the circumstance of failing to grasp the wisdom given by Spiritual masters, both men and women, through the ages, the circumstance of choosing expenditure on arms which result in death, the circumstance of not choosing expenditure on healing our human family. The present days contain Nobel's "force of circumstances" which "will render them (wars) impossible".

Athenian philosopher and disciple of Socrates, Plato (428-348 B.C.) on war: "Without determining as yet whether war does good or harm, this much we may affirm, that now we have discovered war to be derived from causes of almost all the evils in States, private as well as public." Plato, once again on war: "Whence comes wars and fightings, and factions? Whence but from the body and the lusts of the body? Wars are occasioned by the love of money, and money has to be acquired for the same and service of the body."

Notice when Plato lived. Hundreds of years before Christ. Thank Creator/Source that we, with the help of the Holy Spirit, are finally changing paradigms and that the historical models are coming to an end. Anticipate the great changes, which are already beginning, and rejoice that they are happening in your lifetime. Rejoice that you will witness great changes of a magnitude never seen before on this planet. You are witnessing the literal Creation of Heaven on Earth. Human evolution is unending and now we see the evolution of Spiritual consciousness.

British mathematician and philosopher Bertrand Russell (1872-1970) in his book titled "The Future of Mankind" had this to say about war: "If war no longer occupied men's thoughts and energies, we could within a generation, put an end to all serious poverty throughout the

33

world." think about what Russell said there in 1950.

Ask yourself why there are no discussions dealing with war and poverty anywhere to be found on mass media such as television, radio, newspapers and magazines. At risk of being repetitive the reason is that the remnants of the old, historical paradigms where the ego is trusted more than the Spirit still are being used for ego and self. Once the new paradigms are a reality we will see the natural changes where trust in Spirit and concern for others will come into play. Never for a second doubt that these changes are coming as this is being written and will only increase in power. It is humanity's divine destiny.

American poet Carl Sandburg (1878-1967) could be seen as a prophet with his short, famous quote: "Sometime they'll give a war and nobody will come." That sometime is rapidly approaching. Can you imagine how good you are going to feel on that day? The feeling will be the same one those who have had the near death experience returned to describe for us. What these men and women experienced was the Love of the Creator for them. This experience has led these men and women to write books, appear on television and radio talk shows and other avenues to share what happened to them. The experiences were so profound that these men and women had no choice but to share them with us. Find their stories in print and on the internet. You will be blown away and divinely inspired. Their stories are life changing in a good and positive way, for both the people who had the experiences and those who learn from them.

English poet Percy Shelley (1792-1822) was described by fellow English poet Mathew Arnold as "A beautiful and ineffectual angel, beating in the void his luminous wings in vain." Shelley, with the following, shares the vision of Sandburg: "A brighter morn awaits the human day, when poverty and wealth, the thirst of fame, the fear of infamy, disease and woe, war with its million horrors, and fierce hell, shall live but in the memory of time." Shelley wrote these words in 1810 when he was only 18 years old. He did not receive acclaim until after he transitioned to Spirit. He is now considered one the great lyric poets. Just as we considered Sandburg prophetic we consider Shelley prophetic. These words convey this time we are living in now. Once again, rejoice that you are witnessing and experiencing the greatest Spiritual transformation this Earth has ever seen.

American general in the union army William Tecumseh Sherman (1820-1891) honestly shares his thoughts on the experiencing of war: "You cannot qualify war in harsher terms than I will. War is cruelty, and you cannot refine it; and those who brought war into our country deserve all the curses and maledictions a people can pour out." Also, "I am tired and sick of war. Its glory is all moonshine. It is only those who have neither fired a shot nor heard the shrieks and groans of the wounded, who cry aloud for blood. War is hell." And..., "There is many a boy here today who looks on war as all glory, but, boys, it is all hell. You can bear this warning voice to generations yet to come. I look upon war with horror."

How often do we hear our leaders in Washington speak the words like those quoted here? These historical figures were giving us evidence and warning of the consequences of choosing war over Peace. One day soon the entire human race will understand. Thank God that day will be dawning soon.

The man credited with discovering vitamin C, American biochemist, Nobel Prize winner 1937, Albert Szent-Gyorgyi was born in Budapest, Hungary. One more man giving us wisdom and warning: "You have only to wish it and you can have a world without hunger, disease, cancer and toil--anything you wish, wish anything and it can be done. Or else we can exterminate ourselves... At present we are on the road to extermination." Then..., "Man is a very strange animal. In much of the world half the children go to bed hungry and we spend a trillion on rubbish--steel, iron, tanks. We are all criminals. There is an old Hungarian poem, 'If you are among brigands (n. One who lives by plunder usually as a member of a band) and you are silent, you are a brigand yourself.'" And finally..., "It is sad that man is not intelligent enough to solve problems without killing... The present world crisis can be solved only by a general human revolution against outdated concepts... Man is not a blood-thirsty animal, and war is only due to the greed and lust for power of relatively small groups, the conspiracy of the few against the many."

Have you heard words like these anywhere? These are the words of a visionary. The next time you watch an interview of your favorite Hollywood actor/actress, a famous musician, a politician or sports star think about and compare their words to the words contained here. Then, take any of these words/thoughts and write a letter to the editor which includes them. Strike a balance for truth. Call a radio talk show and read them. Share them through e-mails and social media.

Send e-mails to your representative in Congress, your Senator, any Senator, the President. If you have thoughts about an issue and you feel you can contribute with your ideas for real, positive results then do it. What is there to lose? If, and when, your ideas are communicated and received, they very possibly will be part of the solutions. Stop underestimating your ability to bring change in this world. Those who have effected change throughout history were human the same as you. God gave you free will so you can use it for the helping of others. As we help others we help ourselves. As we heal others we heal ourselves.

Russian writer Leo Tolstoy (1828-1910). From his classic novel "War and Peace": "But what is war? What is needed for success in warfare? What are the habits of the military? The aim of war is murder; the methods of war are spying, treachery, and their encouragement, the ruin of a country's inhabitants, robbing them or stealing to provision the army, and fraud and falsehood termed military craft. The habits of the military class are the absence of freedom, discipline, idleness, ignorance, cruelty, debauchery, and drunkenness. And in spite of all this, it is the highest class, respected by everyone... And he who kills most people receives the highest awards."

Fellow Russian writer Maksim Gorki (1868-1936) on Tolstoy: "No man deserves more to be called a genius, no man is more complex, more contradictory, more admirable than he in all things, yes, in all things... He is a man who envelops all men, a man-mankind."

Gandhi considered Tolstoy's non-fiction work "What is Art?" to be Tolstoy's masterpiece. In it Tolstoy states criterion for true art. Amongst other criterion the work must convey the highest Spiritual thought/feeling on the planet. Another is the work must result in a literal improvement in the human condition. We have read "What is Art?" and would recommend it highly. God knows we can use some literal improvement in the human condition.

Finally, on war, we listen again to American social scientist Thorstein Veblen (1857-1929) from "The Theory of the Leisure Class": "The enthusiasm for war, and the predatory temper of which it is the index, prevail in the largest measure among the upper classes, especially among the hereditary leisure class."

The events of September 11, 2001 must be investigated thoroughly, completely and without any omissions. Truth must prevail.

The time has come for war to end. War is the greatest failing of mankind. Very soon the previous statement will be "War was the greatest failing of mankind." Keep faith that a world without war is going to be a reality. In all of your prayers thank God that this reality is one which you will witness in your lifetime. The Spiritual evolution of the human race is happening and will continue to increase in intensity until every man and woman will understand that we are all brothers and sisters on our Mother Earth.

These evolutionary events will be of such a magnitude that time will literally end. Spiritual enlightenment will be of such a high level that a literal Heaven on Earth will be the reality we see before our eyes. Can you feel the anticipation of these coming events increasing day by day? It is coming. There is nothing anyone, anywhere, in any position of power or authority, can do to stop these events. It is the destiny of mankind to evolve spiritually.

Mother Earth Abundance. Food.

Consider how gloriously the Creator of life made Mother Earth with all of her many varieties of food. Think very deeply about all of the different fruits and vegetables that have nourished and sustained life on Earth since time began. Appreciate that these forms of nourishment are Sacred gifts to us and all living things. How many of us take these Sacred gifts for granted and are not truly thankful for them? How many of us pray for our fellow man so that all may be nourished with the gifts of our Creator and Mother Earth?

Mother Earth at this time produces enough food for the entire human population. She produces three times as much food as the human race needs to be nourished properly. Entirely too much of her abundance is wasted instead of being properly distributed to where it is needed. Far too many lands on planet Earth have human beings suffering from hunger and starvation. Solutions to the problems associated with inadequate food are available but sadly not being utilized. Unfortunately the root of the problem is the love of money.

The love of money which results in the hunger and starvation of our brothers and sisters every day on Earth is evidence of Spiritual bankruptcy. When Jesus Christ said, "What you do to the least among you, you do to me." he was referring to those who are suffering hunger and starvation right now on this planet Earth. As the human race continues to ignore our hungry, starving brothers and sisters it ignores Jesus Christ. The Spiritual message here is that we are the family of man and we are all one. When the suffering of our fellow family members is not given the Spiritual importance that the highest Spiritual wisdom calls for, we are then falling short of our potential for achieving unconditional Love.

Unconditional Love is the highest evolutionary state achievable in this life. All of the thought, effort and action taken in this physical realm should have as its basis nothing but unconditional Love. When this highest Love is known by the human race then the thought, effort and action of the men and women on planet Earth will not turn away from suffering but will end that suffering. The roadblocks standing in the way of the elimination of suffering on Earth will be cleared away and a Sacred way of living will become a reality.

At this time, of all the roadblocks in the way of creating a Sacred way of living on Earth, the main roadblock is the genetically modified organism or GMO. The creation of GMO food and the events leading up to its approval for the market are unbelievably saddening to witness. For the human race to take such a giant step away from Sacred life is of such a concern that the feelings of sadness for Mother Earth and all of her inhabitants is indescribable. The genetic manipulations of Sacred life, with recognition of the most extreme consequences coming from the manipulations, are shocking and disturbing at the highest level.

The recognition of this phenomenon called GMO food results in feelings of a nightmarish, hellish degree. The magnitude of the human error resulting in these GMO foods being planted and consumed by humans and all life forms on Earth is unparalleled. Unparalleled action to ban GMO food is required now. Any delay in eliminating this stupendous error will only increase the damage that has been done. The threat to life on Mother Earth coming from GMO food is the highest threat that life on Mother Earth has ever faced.

Let us understand this life threatening error. Corporations create GMO food by genetically altering plants and then patenting the new plant. What public institution would allow the patenting of God given life? We are talking about food; every living thing on this Earth needs food for survival. For human institutions to allow the patenting of life is nothing less than incredible. Jesus Christ said, "Forgive them father. They know not what they do." It is difficult to come to grips with the magnitude of the human error regarding GMO food. It is more difficult to follow Jesus' teaching to forgive in this case. We do forgive those who have committed this monumental error. We pray that the error will be recognized and corrected now. For the sake of Sacred life in this generation and generations to come.

There are a number of corporations involved with genetically modified organisms. Many of you may be aware of the largest corporation involved with selling GMOs, Monsanto. To you reading this who are not aware of the ecological crisis called GMO food go to your computer and Google "Monsanto/GMO food/dangers" and you will be shocked, angered, saddened and extremely concerned. The awareness of the severe consequences of continuing to plant and consume GMO foods will cause a concern in you for Sacred life that you have never experienced before.

Perhaps many of you reading this have heard of Canadian canola farmer Percy Schmeiser. His dealings with Monsanto are well known to all those concerned about GMO foods and will open the eyes of you who are not aware of the GMO crisis.

Percy Schmeiser and his family are from Canada and have been farming for over 50 years, most recently canola. Percy has been involved in Canadian provincial and federal government in the agriculture sector. Let us say to begin that Percy Schmeiser is an international hero and a great man. This man's story, after you hear it, will strain to the limit your belief in the power and rightness of forgiveness. We hope that you will not become too livid after hearing his story but use Spiritual knowledge and wisdom when determining your course of action.

In 1996 GMO food/crops were introduced into the United States of America and Canada. Supporters of the introduction came from the corporations who planned to profit. They said that GMO food/crops would result in better yields, less chemical use and the reduction of hunger and starvation. The process of genetic modification involves taking genes from a separate entity and shooting them into plant cells resulting in a patentable new life form. This could include the crossing of genetic traits from other plants, bacteria or animals. The process begs many questions about the ownership of life such as, "Who is the original owner?", "The plant?", "The indigenous people who have used the plant for generations?"

If you own the patent do you claim responsibility when something goes wrong? The laws pertaining to GMO patents is very muddled. Who is responsible when GMO food contaminates a neighboring farm through gene drift? The first major crops to be genetically modified, government approved and grown were canola, soy, corn and cotton. The approval process utterly failed to determine whether the crops would be safe for human or animal consumption. The government agencies basically used the corporation studies to arrive at their decisions to approve. Improper science included in corporate studies was not given the intense scrutiny required for such a massive action. Government regulatory agency shortcomings in the approval process with regard to scientific studies were very, very unfortunate.

In 1998 Mr. and Mrs. Schmeiser were sued by Monsanto for growing Monsanto canola without a license from Monsanto. The Schmeisers reaction was that Monsanto had contaminated their farm. The Schmeisers had done absolutely nothing. The wind had blown Monsanto canola seed from the neighboring farm onto their farm. During the court case Monsanto admitted that the Schmeisers had never bought or used Monsanto GM canola. The Schmeisers lost the case with the judge saying that, "It did not matter how your farm was contaminated, you cannot use their (Monsanto's) seed. You (Schmeisers) do not own the Monsanto seeds/plants on your farm."

The Schmeisers appealed their case to the federal court of Canada and after spending $300,000 lost again. Imagine what these honorable farming people were going through. Their only chance at that point was to appeal to the Supreme Court of Canada which they did. After five years the Supreme Court of Canada heard the case of Monsanto vs. The Schmeiser farm. In the meantime Monsanto lawyers had sued the Schmeisers for

$1,000,000, their farm and land. Monsanto attempted to take from the Schmeisers their farm so that the Schmeisers could not mortgage their farm in order to have funds to fight Monsanto legally.

The Canadian Supreme Court ruled in favor of the Schmeisers. They had to spend $400,000 to pay for the legal costs. There was no payment made by Monsanto to the Schmeisers for their legal costs. You can imagine what pain and suffering farmers will be forced to go through until this GMO food is banned from the Earth. The question is: "Who owns life?" Life is Sacred, no one should have the right to own life. It is incredible that we as humans have come to this point. Where does the patenting go from here? Will corporations eventually be able to patent human life?

The Schmeisers still had not escaped from having to deal with Monsanto. Monsanto canola had gone onto their farm and they contacted Monsanto to remove the crops. Monsanto faxed a legal contract to the Schmeisers which had a paragraph blacked out. The Schmeisers requested the form be re-faxed without the paragraph being blacked out. The paragraph read, "No one in the Schmeiser family will ever sue Monsanto... The Schmeiser family will not talk about this case to anyone..." The Schmeisers took Monsanto to small claims court and Monsanto was ordered to pay the Schmeisers $640 for their removal of Monsanto canola plants, setting a precedent for GMO corporate liability. The Schmeisers considered the precedent to be a great thing for farmers all around the world.

There is no such thing as containment of GMO crops. It is impossible to prevent GMO crops from travelling by wind, insect or animal to the surrounding environment. This is why it is of the utmost importance that GMO foods be banned as soon as possible. Many of you reading this understand that organic foods are much more nutritious than conventional foods and provide more minerals and vitamins. Organic farming yields 80% more than GMO crops. Organic farming with GMO contamination is threatened. Organic farmers all around the world are extremely concerned about GMO food/crops literally destroying their farms and livelihoods.

The GMO food product we are about to describe requires a preliminary warning to be issued. We pray for your Spiritual, emotional and physical health upon learning of this genetically modified food product. The product is called terminator seed. The seed is one which terminates itself after one planting. The ages old practice since time immemorial of farmers saving their seeds for next year's planting is in jeopardy. The ramifications of terminator seeds are incomprehensible. Thinking about the ramifications is so utterly saddening that one is unable to convey the emotions felt with any words in the human language.

Monsanto GMO cotton has been in India now for a number of years. As opposed to the claims made by supporters of GMO crops such as higher yields, less chemical spraying costs etc. The seed and chemical input costs having to be paid by Indian farmers have increased manifold. Many of these farmers have had to obtain loans from banks in order to save their farms and livelihoods. Many have not been able to earn enough money to keep their farms going and have been destroyed. The combination of being unable to save seeds because of terminator seed technology, and the massive increase in seed and chemical costs, has led to a tremendous number of farmers in India losing their farms.

Terminator seeds are all about total control of the world's food supply. One cannot believe that this state of affairs is a reality on planet Earth at this time. Monsanto and other corporations involved with genetically modified food have spent billions of dollars buying seed companies in order to dominate food production world-wide. There will be no choices, no co-existence and no containment with GMO food/crops. The yields are lower, chemical costs are four times higher and the nutritional yield is 50% lower than traditional food/crops.

There is no benefit to be derived by allowing GMO food/crops to continue. There are nothing but negatives to be seen and felt by humanity through the continued planting of GMO food/crops. GMO food will result in more hunger and starvation on Earth. The social impacts are incalculable.

Percy Schmeiser describes the lengths that Monsanto will go to enforce their patents through legalities. He describes Monsanto's contracts with farmers as vicious, containing gag orders and resulting in the farmers' giving up of all rights. There is small print saying that if you open a bag of Monsanto seed you agree to all terms of Monsanto's patent whether you signed a contract or not. Farmers receive letters from Monsanto where if you tell Monsanto about a neighboring farmer that has Monsanto crops on their farm you will get a free leather jacket.

Monsanto has created an atmosphere of fear in farming communities all around the world. Extortion letters have been mailed where Monsanto demands money from farmers because Monsanto thinks the farmer has their crop. Threats of lawsuits from Monsanto have put farming families through a form of hell as these families worry about their futures and their farms. In the past farmers freely talked and were friendly with their neighbors. This age old

Spirit of community and friendliness has been replaced by distrust and a tearing of the social fabric of farming communities.

Cities around the world are fighting to ban GMO food against Monsanto, Dupont, Syngenta and other corporations. There are countries around the world that have banned GMO food/crops. Most European countries require that food be labeled GMO in order that consumers know what they are buying for their families. There is no GMO labeling requirement in the United States of America. People in America do not know whether the food they are purchasing is GMO food or not although 80% of the people want GMO food labeled.

95% of soy crops are GMO, 70% of the cotton and corn are GMO, sugar beet and alfalfa GMO's have been approved while wheat is in the works. Monsanto and other corporations own 50% of the world's seed supplies. These corporations are motivated by the desire to maximize profits, increase market share and increase control over farmers' abilities to survive and plant what they want. One can use the analogy of the drug dealer when it comes to agribusiness.

Monsanto has sued thousands of farmers since 1996 for "stealing" their patented crops when the farmers did nothing but let the wind blow. Many of you are aware that the defoliant dioxin used in the Vietnam War was made by Monsanto. Dioxin is one of the deadliest chemicals known to man and millions of people were exposed to dioxin in Vietnam. Cancer and genetic defects continue to afflict those exposed to dioxin in the Vietnam War, both in Vietnam and veterans, to this day. Thousands of affected veterans were denied benefits because of falsified scientific studies on the effects of dioxin produced by Monsanto.

Monsanto GMO crops are all around the world and are allowed to be produced and sold because of falsified Monsanto studies. What kind of leaders would allow potentially harmful GMO crops to be grown and sold around the world when they knew that there were questions about their safety? Monsanto has sued and bankrupted farmers who are simply doing God's work of feeding people. They have no guilty conscience after destroying anyone who stands in their way.

These agribusiness monopolies destroy every farmer and community that gets in their paths. The destruction of resources that allow people to live and survive, increases in illness, poverty and death are the ramifications of allowing the scourge of GMO food/crops to continue. In many countries food sovereignty is being taken away, where people must move to cities and find food in garbage cans, when before they grew whatever food and raised whatever animals they needed on their small farms.

GMO foods have been shown to increase health problems associated with the immune system, reproduction and insulin regulation. Roundup herbicide is being flooded onto farmlands in America and around the world. GMO food/crops are a form of genetic roulette. Animal studies have shown GMO food to produce many times the allergens, infertility and birth defects. Many animals will not eat GMO foods.

Scientists who oppose GMO food/crops after discovering safety problems are attacked and suffer retribution for telling their truths. Many of them give up after these attacks, including attacks in the media, take a toll on themselves and their families. Meanwhile one billion people go hungry in the world every day when distribution and poverty are the causes. All of the promises made about GMO foods were not true. GMO food/crops have lower yields, the seeds cost more, the crops require more chemicals, the seeds cannot be saved and the produce tastes no better, if not worse, than non-GMO food/produce.

Regulatory agencies like the Food and Drug Administration (FDA) allow biotech companies to approve GMO foods themselves. The companies use unreliable, falsified data in their scientific studies in order to fix the process of approvals. The biotech industry protects itself from lawsuits as GMO food does not have to be labeled as GMO food. How can a consumer sue for damages caused by GMO food if no one knows whether they consumed GMO food or not? The FDA has been hijacked by food and pharmaceutical companies. An independent body should be formed to investigate safety concerns as effective scientific studies and evidence are in short supply.

Just as the financial industry was allowed to destroy the world's economy the agribusiness industry is being allowed to destroy the world's food supply. Spiritual leadership of the highest caliber is required at this time. There is no other choice for humanity but to put a stop to GMO food/crops.

What kind of legacy are we handing to future generations? Humanity must fight for good safe food for everyone. Humanity must fight for the rights of farmers to produce safe food and re-use their seeds from year to year as the Creator designed. GMO crops will do damage with cross pollination. They will combine with other crops, plants, trees and animals in nature. Terminator seeds are the greatest assault on life that the world has ever seen.

Folks, if you have not by now come to the conclusion that GMO food/crops must be banned, the following will move you to demand that GMO food/crops be banned... Now. We pray that the following statistic does not harm you and that you have the ability to react in the highest Spiritual way. Between 200,000 and 250,000 Indian farmers have committed suicide in the last fifteen years. This is an international scandal of the highest order. We are sorry that we had to give you this information as it is information which is cause for much hurt and suffering. It had to be said as it is a true indication of the absolute severity of this human condition. We had to give you this statistic because it points to the reality which mankind absolutely must look at squarely and responsibly without delay.

The Original Teachings.

In order to provide a contrasting, alternative vision to the harrowing vision of GMO food/crops described, we will share with you the Native American Hopi Indian viewpoint. We pray that you will be strengthened Spiritually by these thoughts and words. The perspectives contained will show a clear contrast to our present Earthly reality. The people of the world must choose between the two perspectives.

We will begin with the Hopi legend of Maasaw. Maasaw is the Hopi God, deity, Spirit who gave the Hopi people their original instructions. Maasaw had only four possessions. They were his digging stick, his seeds, his water and his cloak. Maasaw said, "If you live as I live, you can come and live with me." The message Maasaw was giving to the Hopi and all mankind was a message of simplicity.

How can one describe the life of simplicity? The simple life calls for not taking more for one self than is required. It attempts to avoid misuse and waste of resources. A simple lifestyle is one which contains nothing that is self-serving or selfish. Where is the concern for our brothers and sisters around the world? The survival of humanity depends on our motivation to share this planet's abundance with all. Then the entire planet will walk in beauty.

Make your Spiritual agreement with your Creator, be it God, Great Spirit, Source or Prime Essence. Make your decision to live your life as simply as possible. Make a decision to become as self-sufficient as possible. If you have any unnecessary material things give them to someone who needs them, deny yourself those things not necessary. In any way that you can bring about a relationship with Mother Earth. Begin to regularly celebrate that relationship then you will develop a deeper respect for the rest of Creation. Then you will develop a new attitude toward all of life.

Pray for the purification of yourself and all so that this world will become a Peaceful world.

45

Pray for abundant food, health and happiness for all of Mother Earth's inhabitants. Love all of Creation and then you will find the Creation returning that Love to you. The Hopi people believe that the world's Spiritual center is Hopi land. To those who own the trained mind and sight world changes will be visible in Hopi land.

The following Hopi prayer was delivered to the United Nations General Assembly along with the United Nations People's Assembly. Imagine what this Earth will be like when all live in accord with the honorable Spirit of this prayer's words.

"Great Spirit and all unseen, this day we pray and ask you for guidance, humbly we ask you to help us and fellowmen to have recourse to Peaceful ways of life, because of uncontrolled deceitfulness by humankind. Help us all to Love, not hate one another. We ask you to be seen in an image of Love and Peace. Let us be seen in beauty, the colors of the rainbow. We respect our Mother, the planet, with our loving care, for from her breast we receive our nourishment. Let us not listen to the voices of the two-hearteds, the destroyers of mind, the haters and self-made leaders, whose lusts for power and wealth will lead us into confusion and darkness..."

"...Seek visions always of world beauty, not violence nor battlefield. It is our duty to pray always for harmony between man and Earth, so that the Earth will bloom once more. Let us show our emblem of Love and goodwill for all life and land. Pray for the house of glass (the United Nations), for within it are minds clear and pure as ice and mountain streams. Pray for the leaders of nations in the house of mica who in their own quiet ways help keep the Earth in balance. We pray the Great Spirit that one day our Mother Earth will be purified into a healthy, Peaceful one. Let us sing for strength of wisdom with all nations for the good of the people. Our hope is not yet lost, purification must occur to restore the health of our Mother Earth for lasting Peace and happiness. Techqua Ikachi."

Find it in yourself to bring about a real, reverent attitude toward all life and the environment of the Earth. The Creator wants to rescue us, so we must rescue the world. When you pray make your prayer be for the well being of the world. Try to remember to always use good words when talking with or about people. Stop yourself from ever saying words which are harmful or hurtful. Come to the point where you have respect for yourself, for others, for all things and the Mother Earth herself.

Understand that Mother Earth is a living organism just as we all are. For that reason she responds to our thoughts. Once this attitude of oneness and Peace is accepted by the entire world, all will work together and accomplish great things. Future generations will see this time as the one where the greatest accomplishments in human history were made reality. The Hopi were to be watchful. "The most important factor we were instructed to watch is mankind because he will become the most mindless and heedless foe of Earth and nature." Mankind must be watchful of its actions. "The present crises of world events is an unfoldment of life cycles which we set in motion through our own behavior."

"Let your hearts be filled with happiness, enjoy your lives to the fullest, for this is the best medicine for sickness. Live long, for there are great and exciting adventures awaiting you. So time passes on, and the prophecies handed down by our ancient people begin to unfold. Many great events lie before us, and we are witnessing with astonishment today the fact that our ancients' words were right."

"Often we are sad and discouraged that our voices are not being heard, so we try not to grieve. Instead, we gather strength from the teaching we learned: that we must neither lose sight of our prayers or the divine laws of the Creator, laws which never change or break down, that often bring miracles when one meets obstacles which seem impossible to pass. For better or worse we must struggle on until our prophecies are fulfilled."

"The wisdom accumulated by anyone who is willing to stand up and be counted is respected. Anyone with a strong Spirit and strength who is unafraid of reaching our goal of destiny, which is for the good of the Earth and all life, can understand the tasks involved, and can count on support from others. There is a saying, if one or two be strong, three or four will be greater under the banner of the Great Creator.

For years, the Hopi elders say, "Our founding fathers have passed the knowledge of survival from mouth to mouth, which is to respect all living things, for we are all one and created by one. It seems like now people have forgotten this concept of the right way of survival. They have replaced it with defensive tactics, and as a result are always running behind. They are racing steadily downhill to ruins. We mean that all nations on Earth are doing this. People must skid to a stop and look around. There might be a dried-up old root (Hopi elder) visible near you; get hold of it for support until you see the light."

Notes

Monetary Systems.

All we can say to you is, "Oh, my God!" when beginning this section on money and the printing of currencies by private banks around planet Earth. For those of you reading this that have an understanding of the international monetary system and how it operates, the "Oh, my God!" moment has already occurred. For those of you reading this who have yet to gain an understanding of the monetary system, you will be experiencing the "Oh, my God!" moment as well.

The importance of understanding the way money is created and by whom is of the highest urgency at this time in human history. It cannot be stressed strongly enough just how important this issue is to every man, woman and child on this planet Earth right now. Genetically modified food and the world financial system are the most important issues that mankind must deal with at this time. Let us repeat this so you understand totally: there are no more important issues.

Everyone on this planet must become aware of both the historical and present realities of this worldwide monetary system. If you are aware of the realities you must do something to change them. When you become aware of these realities you must do something to change them. There is no choice but for the changes to be made. Change, you can rest assured must come and soon. Change, you can also rest assured, will come and soon.

The state of affairs regarding the international financial situation has reached the point where it simply has become untenable (untenable adj. 1. being such that defense or maintenance is impossible). The damage that has been done has been incalculable. The damage done has been simply beyond comprehension. The damage done has reached such a high level that it is for all practical purposes inevitable that the awareness of this issue will become the most important story on Earth.

Thank God that the change is coming and that the arrival of the change is at hand.

Banker Mayer Amschel Rothschild said in 1790: "Let me issue and control a nation's money and I care not who writes the laws."

If you ask most people "What is the federal reserve?" the typical response would be something like "Oh, that's the part of the government that prints the money" or "they're in Washington; they print the money". Most people believe that the federal reserve system is a branch of the United States government. Most believe the federal reserve is a public, hence, non-profit institution. Those of you who have not yet had your "Oh, my God!" moment, understand. The federal reserve is not a part of the United States government. The federal reserve system is a collection of private banks. Private, not public. For-profit, not non-profit. This is the first fact that you absolutely must understand.

We will take the journey into this slowly. We will come to the end of this journey well aware of the gravity involved for human beings everywhere. Take your time. What we are trying to do here is increase your awareness to the point where action is seen as not just necessary, but demanded. We pray that the following information will not, because is it so shocking, hurt you in any way. The information describes the reality which we as humanity are living and experiencing at this time.

Let us begin our journey with some general thoughts from history about money. We will look at words from historical figures. There has been a kind of war, if you will, going on for hundreds of years between private bankers and those opposed to them. The central reason for this war has been, and is, who will control the issue of the currency. The battles have been fought, and are now fought, throughout the centuries in virtually every country on Earth. Let us look at some historical quotes/thoughts to get a feel and start the discussion.

Anacreon (568-478 B.C.) Greek lyric poet:

"Cursed he be above all others who is enslaved by love of money. Money takes the place of brothers, money takes the place of parents, money brings us to war and slaughter."

Sophocles (496-406 B.C.) Greek tragic poet:

"Of all the foul growths current in the world, the worst is money. Money drives men from home, plunders proud cities, and perverts honest minds to shameful practice, godlessness and crime."

Socrates (470-399 B.C.) Greek stonemason, general, philosopher:

"Are you not ashamed of heaping up in the greatest amount of money and honor and reputation, and caring so little about wisdom and truth and the greatest improvement of the soul, which you never regard or heed at all?'

Diogenes (400-325 B.C.) Greek philosopher:

"Love of money is the Mother of all evils."

Aristotle (384-322 B.C.) Greek philosopher:

"Money was intended to be used in exchange, but not to increase at interest, which means the birth of money from money, is applied to the breeding of money... Of all modes of getting wealth this is the most unnatural."

Terence (190-159 B.C.) Latin playwright:

"How unjust it is, that they who have but little should be always adding something to the wealth of the rich."

Francis Bacon (1561-1626) English essayist, philosopher:

"Above all things, good policy is to be used that the treasure and monies in state be not gathered into few hands... And money is like muck, no good except it be spread."

Thomas Fuller (1654-1734) English clerk:

"The pleasures of the rich are bought with the tears of the poor."

Voltaire (1694-1778) French philosopher:

"In general, the art of government consists in taking as much money as possible from one class of citizens and to give it to the other."

John C. Calhoun (1782-1850) American Statesman:

"A power has risen up in the government greater than the people themselves, consisting of many, and various, and powerful interests, combined into one mass, and held together by the cohesive power of the vast surplus in the banks."

Washington Irving (1783-1859) American writer:

"Almighty dollar."

George Bernard Shaw (1856-1950) Irish dramatist:

"The seven deadly sins... Food, clothing, firing, rent, taxes, respectability and children. Nothing can lift these seven millstones from man's neck but money; and the Spirit cannot soar until the millstones are lifted."

Andre Suares (1868-1948) French writer:

"As one wages war with the blood of others, so one makes a fortune with the money of others."

Woodrow Wilson (1856-1924) American President:

"The great monopoly in this country is the money monopoly. So long as it exists, our old variety of freedom and individual energy of development are out of the question."

So we have a sense that the money issue has been with us a very long time. Why are we making this attempt to reach people with this information? This is a question which should be thought about as we all have our particular reasons for every action taken. Perhaps it has to do with our agreement with the Spiritual philosophy of the Native American. The Spiritual philosophy which deals with the seven generations. One who accepts this philosophy comes to a point where the consideration of the effects of any action keeps the seventh generation in mind. Every action must not result in any negative consequences for those coming seven generations into the future. The actions must be seen to either do no harm or improve the conditions for those coming seven generations from now.

If this seventh generation philosophy of Spirituality were common and practiced seven generations ago, then we would not see ourselves in the present unfortunate situation. Those who took the actions seven generations ago would have chosen other actions; actions which would have helped their fellow human brothers and sisters instead of manipulating them. Unfortunately the choices made were those which failed to take the well-being of humanity into consideration. If we understand that all life and all things are Sacred then we cannot willfully do harm. We must fight the urge to look for revenge when we understand what has been happening for hundreds of years. Anger is never called for however difficult it is to not feel the emotion. Humanity has simply committed error through the centuries. First forgive, then correct the error.

These historical and continuing errors must and will be corrected. They will be corrected because the human race has come to see them as errors. We will be at a Spiritual level where these corrections will occur naturally. There will simply be no way not to make the corrections because we understand that not to do so would result in harm to our brothers and sisters in the human family. So have no doubt that we the human race are improving our condition at a rapid pace. Our collective future is one that is going to evidence the common experience of Love, Peace, justice, fairness and happiness.

America along with all other countries on Earth that use debt-based monetary systems have been, and are now being, robbed blind. The root cause has to be understood. Fully understood. National debts occur when governments spend more than they take in with taxes. In the United States the government then issues United States government bonds. Government bonds equal debt. Let us look at how we arrived at this sad state of affairs.

In 1934 Robert Hemphill, credit manager of the federal reserve bank of Atlanta said, "Someone has to borrow every dollar we have in circulation... If the banks create ample money we are prosperous; if not, we starve. When one gets a complete grasp of the picture, the tragic absurdity of our hopeless position is... incredible. It is the most important subject intelligent persons can investigate and reflect upon."

The United States government can issue all the money it needs. At present all of our money is created out of debt. What is the reason that we the people of the United States have not heard of this? What the government cannot raise in taxes it must borrow from the private banks of the federal reserve. The government recently actually borrowed one trillion dollars and then turned around and gave it to the banks in the form of bailouts. Could those in Congress actually be ignorant of what is happening? You cannot borrow yourself out of debt; you cannot drink yourself sober.

Most citizens do not understand what the root cause of the debt problem is. Most citizens do not understand there is a problem. The battle for the control of the monetary system has been going on for hundreds of years. You will not read about the battle in your history books.

The only time Jesus Christ got angry was when he confronted the moneychangers. When coming upon the moneychangers "He made a whip out of cords and... He scattered the coins of the moneychangers and overturned their tables." Passage (John 2:15) of the Holy Bible. The moneychangers were the bankers of their day and they were stealing from the poor. An assassination attempt was made on President Andrew Jackson while he received numerous death threats. Presidents Abraham Lincoln, James Garfield and John Kennedy may all have been assassinated because of their pushing of monetary reforms. Is it possible that Jesus Christ was assassinated for confronting the moneychangers? The bankers of their day? Think about it. For the love of money is the root of all evil.

Representative from Alabama Howard Milford wrote "the American Plutocracy" in 1895. An excerpt reads, "Without the use of either gold or silver, Rome became mistress of the commerce of the world. Her people were the bravest, the most prosperous, the most happy, for they knew no grinding poverty. Her money was issued directly to the people, and was composed of a cheap material-copper and brass-based alone upon the faith and credit of the nation. With this abundant money supply she built her magnificent courts and temples. She distributed her lands among the people in small holdings, and wealth poured into the coffers of Rome..."

How things have changed. Julius Caesar changed the monetary system after that, when he brought the gold money for the very rich. Caesar was assassinated, the copper/brass money was taken out of circulation and a depression was the result. So the monetary system battles go back a very long way.

Around the year 1100 A.D. the bankers were the goldsmiths. If they chose to make the gold money plentiful, the economy was good. If they chose to make the gold money scarce, the inevitable depression would occur with the goldsmiths able to buy up the people's assets for pennies on the dollar. Yes, the monetary system battles go back a very long way.

At this point we make a personal observation. As we mentioned earlier, we pray that this information in no way hurts you. It is information which could, obviously, be the source of discouragement and depression. But fear not. Help is on the way. This unfortunate monetary situation the world's people are struggling with will be changed and soon.

The bank of England was founded in 1694 and the bankers asserted their control of the manipulation of England's money quantity. One of the members of the bank of England, William Paterson (1658-1719), "The bank hath benefit of interest on all monies which it creates out of nothing." What a straight ahead statement that was. The bank lent the government of England the money for their wars to the point where 75% of English tax revenues were for interest payments on war bonds. It seems war is good, earns a tidy profit, for those who lend money to the governments who fight them. The only word that comes to mind is hideous (adj. Repulsive, especially to the sight, revoltingly ugly). Citizens and nations became more and more indebted to banks as things went from bad to worse.

The war for independence in America was all about money and who controls its creation. The colonists were determined to, and eventually did, break free of the private banks of England. Why does it seem that none of us came across this fact of America's war for independence in any of our history books? Benjamin Franklin said the following. "Experience, more prevalent than all the logic in the world, has fully convinced us all, that it (paper money issued directly by government) has been, and is now of the greatest advantages to the country." The government having no interest to pay to anyone is the crux of the matter.

So in the year 1764 the parliament of Britain passed a law where taxes had to be paid with gold backed money. This did not sit well with the colonists. Americans were angry and did everything they could to get around England's gold-backed monetary system. Americans were forced to buy everything using only England's gold-backed money. Revolution began in 1775. How many of us are aware that the American war of independence was over the control of the monetary system. Did anyone read about this in their American history books?

One more war in the long line of wars fought over money, power, natural resources and control. Wars with their killing, maiming and incalculable negative consequences. If only the human race could have learned the golden rule, "Do unto others as you would have done to you" hundreds of years ago there would be no need for these writings. Unfortunately these writings are necessary even though the human race is experiencing a raising of consciousness at this time. The word must go out in order that every man, woman and child on Earth experiences the same rise in Spiritual consciousness.

The First Bank of the United States came in 1782 and eventually got a 20 year charter to control the quantity of the money supply for the nation. Thomas Jefferson said, "I wish it were possible to obtain a single amendment to our constitution... Taking from the federal government the power of borrowing." Jefferson also said, "This institution (private-owned central banks) is one of the most deadly hostility against the principles of our constitution... Suppose a series of emergencies should occur... An institution like this... In a critical moment might overthrow the government."

Jefferson also said the following words in 1815 which drives the point firmly home, "The treasury, lacking confidence in the country, delivered itself bound hand and foot to bold and bankrupt adventurers and bankers pretending to have money, whom it could have crushed at any moment... These jugglers were at the feet of government. For it was not any confidence in their frothy bubbles, but the lack of all other money, which induced... People to take their paper... We are now without any common measure of value of property, and private fortunes are up or down at the will of the worst of our citizens... As little seems to be known of the principles of political economy as if nothing had ever been written or practiced on the subject."

Think about these, Thomas Jefferson's words, deeply, as the current federal reserve bank's charter comes up for renewal in the year 2013. We are going to make a prediction. We believe the prediction will come true. The American people will come to a full awareness of the importance of this issue, that monetary reform will be the only choice, without alternative.

We will take a look at some words of second President John Adams (1735-1826), "All the perplexities, confusion and distress in America rise, not from defects in their constitution or confederation, not from want of honor or virtue, so much as from downright ignorance of the nature of coin, credit and circulation." Adams' quote points to the need for all Americans to become informed on monetary policy and the immediate need for monetary reform.

Thank God that once the American people become informed on monetary policy they will adopt the Spirit that during the revolutionary war George Washington conveyed when addressing his troops in 1776, "The fate of unborn millions will now depend, under God, on the courage and conduct of this army... We have, therefore, to resolve to conquer or die." This Spirit will be essential in the winning of this final war to defeat debt slavery on this planet once and for all.

Central, private banks gained a 20 year charter in 1791 to issue the nation's currency. In 1811 the 20 year charter was up for renewal. England, in no uncertain terms, threatened war if the renewal was not successful. The charter was not renewed. Five months later the War of 1812 began. Jefferson had it right. Congress and only Congress should be issuing the nation's currency at no interest to anyone. Jefferson said, "And I sincerely believe, with you, that banking establishments are more dangerous than standing armies; and that the principle of spending money to be paid by posterity, under the name of funding, is but swindling futurity on a large scale."

In 1816 the banks were back in control. Jefferson said, "The treasury, lacking confidence in the country, delivered itself bound hand and foot to bold and bankrupt... Bankers pretending to have money, whom it could have crushed at any moment..." Despite Jefferson, a new 20 year charter was given to the 2nd Bank of the United States in 1816. The English debt-money system was back in place

History moves on to 1832 and an American hero Andrew Jackson. Andrew Jackson ran for the presidency in 1832 with his campaign slogan being "Jackson and no bank". He was determined to rid the country of the private, debt-based banks along with their control of the issuing of currency. We will include a number of President Jackson's quotes at this point as he was among those who most strongly fought the elite. During his office a charter was passed by Congress which Jackson vetoed.

Jackson stated in 1832, "It is maintained by some that the bank is a means of executing the constitutional power 'to coin money and regulate the value thereof... Congress have established a mint to coin money and passed laws to regulate the value thereof. The money so coined, with its value so regulated, and such foreign coins as Congress may adopt are the only currency known to the constitution. But if they have other power to regulate the currency, it was conferred to be exercised by themselves, and not to be transferred to a corporation. If the bank be established for that purpose, with a charter unalterable without its consent, Congress have parted with their power for a term of years, during which the constitution is a dead letter. It is neither necessary nor proper to transfer its legislative power to such a bank, and therefore unconstitutional."

In 1835 after removing government deposits from Rothschild banks an assassination attempt on Jackson was unsuccessful. Jackson claimed banking interests were responsible for the attempt.

The bankers threatened a depression unless Jackson's veto was overturned. Nicholas Biddle, head of the 2nd Bank of the United States, then undertook a series of actions which contracted the money supply. Biddle made good on his promise. The money supply was restricted and a deep depression ensued, with the American people suffering with the typical, bank-induced, pain of unemployment, foreclosures and loss of assets to those ready to buy up for pennies on the dollar.

President Jackson's words in reply reflect a righteous indignation virtually invisible in today's Washington: "You are a den of vipers! I intend to rout (n. An overwhelming defeat) you out, and by the eternal God I will rout you out!" Fortunately for those of that time period the newspapers sided with President Jackson and the bank was not re-chartered. President Jackson succeeded in throwing the financial elite owned central bank out of America.

President Jackson was one of the few American Presidents who attempted and succeeded in returning the power to control the money supply quantity to the people, with the government. Jackson, in his 1837 farewell address said, "...The mischief springs from the power which the moneyed interest derives from a paper currency which they are able to control, from the multitude of corporations with exclusive privileges which they have succeeded in obtaining... And unless you become more watchful in your States and check this Spirit of monopoly and thirst for exclusive privileges you will in the end find that the most important powers of government have been given or bartered away, and the control of your dearest interests have been passed into the hands of these corporations."

We move forward to 1861 and the election of the 16th President Abraham Lincoln. France stationed troops in Mexico and England stationed them in Canada. The American civil war was about to begin with France and England ready to feed on the remains. Lincoln was forced into war by the financial houses of Europe. The European financial houses' plan was to split the United States in two. Divide and conquer.

President Lincoln went to the New York banks for loans to fight the war. The New York banks offered deals for loans with interest rates ranging from 24-36%. Lincoln was dejected. Congressman E.G. Spaulding said in 1862, "Why then should we go into Wall Street, State Street, Chestnut Street, or any other street, begging for money? Their money (private banks) is not as secure as government money... I am unwilling that this government should be left in the hands of any class of men, bankers or moneylenders, however respectable or patriotic they may be. The government is much stronger than any of them." (excerpt from Spaulding speech addressed to Congress in favor of the greenback rather than government borrowing)

But then President Lincoln decided the government would print $450,000,000 worth of "greenbacks", which the government proceeded to do. These were United States notes, all created with no interest for the federal government to have to pay to anyone. Debt-free money which Lincoln successfully used to pay the troops, buy supplies etc. The New York banks wanted to charge the high interest rates to the government for the financing of the civil war. The government found the solution with the printing of the greenbacks.

In 1902 M.I.T. Economics Professor David Rich Dewey wrote on the "greenbacks", "the underlying idea in the greenback philosophy... Is that the issue of currency is a function of the government, a sovereign right which ought not to be delegated to corporations."

A sovereign right? The definition of sovereign: (n, 1. One that exercises supreme, permanent authority, especially in a nation or other governmental unit). Folks, there would be no national debt if the United States government and people had chosen to issue their own currency from the beginning. All countries on Earth would have no national debt if the governments and the people of each respective country had chosen to issue their own currency from their beginnings.

To illustrate the international nature of the monetary issue, Lincoln found an ally in Russia. Alexander II, Tsar of Russia (1855-1881) was having his own problems with the banks of Rothschild. The Rothschilds' wanted to set up central banks in Russia. Alexander II refused them. The Tsar delivered orders to the effect that if England or France intervened in the American civil war for the southern state that Russia would consider the actions a declaration of war on Russia and would side with President Lincoln. The Tsar sent a fleet to America to show he was not bluffing.

In 1865, very near to the time when the civil war ended, President Lincoln was assassinated. He was 56 years old. Can we imagine what more this great leader could have accomplished if not gunned down? Can we fathom a guess for the motive? It is one of the great mysteries of life when those who make the greatest effort to help their fellow man get killed for their efforts.

The American people were getting used to the use of the "greenbacks", the debt-free money which President Lincoln initiated. In 1866 after Lincoln's assassination a money contraction began and Congress began taking the "greenbacks" out of circulation. Then began a series of recessions. There are a number of excellent documentaries available on the internet that give viewers the truth about the history of monetary systems.

Here is a quote from the 1980 "The Truth in Money Book" by Theodore Thoren. It reads, "The hard times which occurred after the civil war could have been avoided if the greenback legislation had continued as President Lincoln had intended. Instead there was a series of "money panics", what we call recessions-which put pressure on Congress to enact legislation to place the banking system under centralized control".

We move on to the year 1873 and what monetary experts call the "Crime of 1873". Around the year of 1873 silver was removed as a form of money. The American people were angry about this and riots resulted. Minnesota Congressman Charles Lindbergh wrote a book in 1913 titled "Banking and Currency and the Money Trust". It deals with the bankers of 1873 efforts to stop the return of the "greenbacks". The following excerpt from Lindbergh's book is a 1877 letter by James Buel, then secretary of the American Bankers Association, to the country's association bankers.

The excerpt reads, (Buel to member bankers) "It is advisable to do all in your power to sustain such prominent daily and weekly newspapers, especially the agricultural and religious press, as will oppose the greenback issue of paper money... To repeal the act creating bank notes, or to restore to circulation the government issue of money will be to provide the people with money and will therefore seriously affect our individual profits as bankers and lenders... See your Congressman at once and engage him to support our interests that we may control legislation." Today's equivalent would be the internal e-mail. Lindbergh's writing is very revealing.

Whoever controls the volume of money. How about the United States sovereign government for a change? Debt free with no interest for a change? How about the end of national debt for a change? Our guess is that you answered the previous three questions with a yes. It is coming. Do not doubt. Given the economic crisis of the late 2000's, there are increasing calls from the public for change. Folks simply know in their guts that there is something crooked going on in the financial sector of this country as well as the entire world.

The next period of American history we will look at is during the years 1880-1900. We will begin with William Jennings Bryan (1860-1925), a Nebraska Congressman, free silver advocate and three time Presidential candidate. He was widely known as "the lion of the free silver movement". His speech at the Democratic convention in Chicago in 1896 titled "Crown of Thorns, Cross of Gold" is regarded as the most powerful political speech ever delivered by many political scientists. The following is the full text of William Jennings Bryan's powerful convention speech of 1896. The speech propelled him to the Democratic nomination for President of the United States at the age of 36.

The Democratic party in 1896 had its gold proponents and its silver proponents. The majority of the delegates to the 1896 Democratic convention were proponents of silver. Up to the point where Bryan delivered his famous speech no-one had effectively spoken for the silver cause, which the delegation overwhelmingly supported. The silver men knew they would be victorious in this fight. They just needed someone to tell them and the gold men why they must put silver at the heart of the platform. Before Bryan took the podium the pump was not just primed, but ready for an explosion. There was the highest form of anticipation in the convention hall as Bryan stepped up to the podium...

Notes

The most famous speech in American political history. William Jennings Bryan on July 9, 1896 at the Democratic national convention in Chicago.

The Cross of Gold.

"It would be presumptuous, indeed, to present myself against the distinguished gentlemen to whom you have listened if this were but a measuring of ability; but this is not a contest among persons. The humblest citizen in all the land when clad in the armor of a righteous cause is stronger than all the whole hosts of error that they can bring. I come to speak to you in the defense of a cause as Holy as the cause of liberty-the cause of humanity. When this debate is concluded, a motion will be made to lay upon the table the resolution offered in commendation of the administration and also the resolution in condemnation of the administration. I shall object to bringing this question down to a level of persons. The individual is but an atom; he is born, he acts, he dies; but principles are eternal; and this has been a contest of principle..."

..."Never before in the history of this country has there been witnessed such a contest as that through which we have passed. Never before in the history of American politics has a great issue been fought out as this issue has been by the voters themselves..."

..."On the 4th of March, 1895, a few democrats, most of them members of Congress, issued an address to the democrats of the nation asserting that the money question was the paramount issue of the hour; asserting also the right of a majority of the Democratic party to control the position of the party on this paramount issue; concluding with the request that all believers in the free coinage of silver in the Democratic party should organize and take charge of and control the policy of the Democratic party..."

..."Three months later, at Memphis, an organization was perfected, and the silver democrats went forth openly and boldly and courageously proclaiming their belief and declaring that if successful they would crystallize in a platform the declaration which they had made; and then began the conflict with a zeal approaching the zeal which inspired the crusaders who followed Peter the Hermit. Our silver democrats went forth from victory to victory, until they are assembled now, not to discuss, not to debate, but to enter up the judgment rendered by the plain people of this country..."

..."But in this contest, brother has been arrayed against brother, and father against son. The warmest ties of Love and acquaintance and association have been disregarded. Old leaders have been cast aside when they refused to give expression to the sentiments of those whom

62

they would lead, and new leaders have sprung up to give direction to this cause of freedom. Thus has the contest been waged, and we have assembled here under as binding and solemn instructions as were ever fastened upon the representatives of a people..."

..."We do not come as individuals. Why, as individuals we might have been glad to compliment the gentleman from New York [Senator Hill], but we knew that the people for whom we speak would never be willing to put him in a position where he could thwart the will of the Democratic party. I say it was not a question of persons; it was a question of principle; and it is not with gladness my friends, that we find ourselves brought into conflict with those who are now arrayed on the other side. The gentleman who just preceded me [Governor Russell] spoke of the old state of Massachusetts. Let me assure him that not one person in all this convention entertains the least hostility to the people of the state of Massachusetts..."

..."But we stand here representing people who are the equals before the law of the largest cities in the state of Massachusetts. When you come before us and tell us that we shall disturb your business interests, we reply that you have disturbed our business interests by your action. We say to you that you have made too limited in its application the definition of a businessman..."

..."The man who is employed for wages is as much a businessman as his employer. The attorney in a country town is as much a businessman as the corporation counsel in a great metropolis. The merchant at the crossroads street is as much a businessman as the merchant of New York. The farmer who goes forth in the morning and toils all day, begins in the spring and toils all summer, and by the application of brain and muscle to the natural resources of this country creates wealth, is as much a businessman as the man who goes upon the board of trade and bets upon the price of grain. The miners who go 1,000 feet into the Earth or climb 2,000 feet upon the cliffs and bring forth from their hiding places the precious metals to be poured in the channels of trade are as much businessman as the few financial magnates who in a backroom corner the money of the world..."

..."We come to speak for this broader class of businessmen. Ah, my friends, we say not one word against those who live upon the Atlantic coast; but those hardy pioneers who braved all the dangers of the wilderness, who have made the desert to blossom as the rose-those pioneers away out there, rearing their children near to nature's heart, where they can mingle their voices with the voices of the birds-out there where they have erected schoolhouses for the education of their children and churches where they praise their Creator, and the cemeteries where sleep the ashes of their dead-are as deserving of the consideration of this party as any people in this country..."

..."It is for these that we speak. We do not come as aggressors. Our war is not a war of conquest. We are fighting in the defense of our homes, our families, and posterity. We have petitioned, and our petitions have been scorned. We have entreated, and our entreaties have been disregarded. We have begged, and they have mocked when our calamity came. We beg no longer; we entreat no more; we petition no more. We defy them! The gentleman from Wisconsin has said he fears a Robespierre. My friend, in this land of the free you need fear no tyrant who will spring up from among the people. What we need is an Andrew Jackson to stand as Jackson stood, against the encroachments of aggregated wealth..."

..."They say that this platform was made to catch votes. We reply to them that changing conditions make new issues; that the principles upon which rest democracy are as everlasting as the hills; but that they must be applied to new conditions as they arise. Conditions have arisen and we are attempting to meet those conditions. They tell us that the income tax ought not to be brought in here; that is not a new idea. They criticize us for our criticism of the Supreme Court of the United States. My friends, we have made no criticism. We have simply called attention to what you know. If you want criticisms, read the dissenting opinions of the court. That will give you criticisms..."

..."They say we passed an unconstitutional law. I deny it. The income tax was not unconstitutional when it was passed. It was not unconstitutional when it went before the Supreme Court for the first time. It did not become unconstitutional until one judge changed his mind; and we cannot be expected to know when a judge will change his mind. The income tax is a just law. It simply intends to put the burdens of government justly upon the backs of the people. I am in favor of an income tax. When I find a man who is not willing to pay his fair share of the burden of the government which protects him, I find a man who is unworthy to enjoy the blessings of a government like ours..."

..."He says that we are opposing the national bank currency. It is true. If you will read what Thomas Benton said, you will find that he said that in searching history he could find but one parallel for Andrew Jackson. That was Cicero, who destroyed the conspiracies of Cataline and saved Rome. He did for Rome what Jackson did when he destroyed the bank conspiracy and saved America. We say in our platform that we believe that the right to coin money and issue money is a function of government. We believe it. We believe it is a part of sovereignty and can no more with safety be delegated to private individuals than can the power to make penal statutes or levy laws for taxation..."

..."Mr. Jefferson, who was once regarded as good Democratic authority, seems to have a different opinion from the gentleman who has addressed us on the part of the minority. Those who are opposed to this proposition tell us that the issue of paper money is a function of the bank and that the government ought to go out of the banking business. I stand with Jefferson rather than with them, and tell them, as he did, that the issue of money is a function of the government and that the banks should get out of the governing business..."

..."They complain about the plank which declares against the life tenure in office. They have tried to strain it to mean that which it does not mean. What we oppose in that plank is the life tenure that is being built up in Washington which establishes an office-holding class and excludes from participation in the benefits the humbler members of our society. Let me call attention to two or three great things. The gentleman from New York says that he will propose an amendment providing that this change in our law shall not effect contracts which, according to the present laws, are made payable in gold..."

..."If he means to say that we cannot change our monetary system without protecting those who have loaned money before the change was made, I want to ask him where, in law or in morals, he can find authority for not protecting the debtors when the Act of 1873 was passed when he now insists that we must protect the creditor. He says he also wants to amend this platform so as to provide that if we fail to maintain the parity within a year that we will then suspend the coinage of silver. We reply that when we advocate a thing which we believe will be successful we are not compelled to raise a doubt as to our own sincerity by trying to show what we will do if we are wrong..."

..."I ask him, if he will apply his logic to us, why he does not apply it to himself? He says that he wants this country to secure an international agreement. Why doesn't he tell us what he is going to do if they fail to secure an international agreement? There is more reason for him to do that than for us to expect to fail to maintain the parity. They have tried for thirty years-thirty years-to secure an international agreement, and those who are waiting for it most patiently who don't want it at all..."

..."Now, my friends, let me come to the great paramount issue. If they ask us here why it is we say more on the money question than we say upon the tariff question, I reply that if protection has slain its thousands the gold standard has slain its tens of thousands. If they ask us why we did not embody all these things in our platform which we believe, we reply to them that when we have restored the money of the constitution, all other necessary reforms will be possible, and that until that is done there is no reform that can be accomplished..."

..."Why is it that within three months such a change has come over the sentiments of the country? Three months ago, when it was confidently asserted that those who believed in the gold standard would frame our platforms and nominate our candidates, even the advocates of the gold standard did not think that we could elect a President; but they had good reasons for the suspicion, because there is scarcely a state here today asking for the gold standard that is not within the absolute control of the republican party..."

..."But note the change. Mr. McKinley was nominated at St. Louis upon a platform that declared for the maintenance of the gold standard until it should be changed into bimetallism by an international agreement. Mr. McKinley was the most popular man among the republicans; and everybody three months ago in the republican party prophesied his election. How is it today? Why, that man who used to boast that he looked like Napoleon, that man shudders today when he thinks that he was nominated on the anniversary of the battle of Waterloo. Not only that, but as he listens he can hear with ever increasing distinctness the sound of the waves as they beat upon the lonely shores of St. Helena..."

..."Why this change? Ah, my friends, is not the change evident to anyone who will look at the matter? It is because no private character, however pure, no personal popularity, however great, can protect from the avenging wrath of an indignant people the man who will either declare that he is in favor of fastening the gold standard upon this people, or who is willing to surrender the right of self-government and place legislative control in the hands of foreign potentates and powers..."

..."We go forward confident that we shall win. Why? Because upon the paramount issue in this campaign there is not a spot of ground upon which the enemy will dare to challenge battle. Why, if they tell us that the gold standard is a good thing, we point to their platform and tell them that their platform pledges the party to get rid of a gold standard and substitute bimetallism. If the gold standard is a good thing, why try to get rid of it? If the gold standard, and I might call your attention to the fact that some of the very people who are in this convention today and tell you that we ought to declare in favor of international bimetallism and thereby declare that the gold standard is wrong and that the principles of bimetallism are better-these very people four months ago were open and avowed advocates of the gold standard and telling us that we could not legislate two metals together even with all the world..."

..."I want to suggest this truth, that if the gold standard is a good thing we ought to declare in favor of its retention and not in favor of abandoning it; and if the gold standard is a bad thing, why should we wait until some other nations are willing to help us let it go? Here is the line of battle. We care not upon which issue they force the fight. We are prepared to meet them on either issue or on both. If they tell us that the gold standard is the standard of civilization, we reply to them that this, the most enlightened of all nations of the Earth, has never declared for a gold standard, and both the parties this year are declaring against it..."

..."If the gold standard is the standard of civilization, why, my friends, should we not have it? So if they come to meet us on that, we can present the history of our nation. More than that, we can tell them this, that they will search the pages of history in vain to find a single instance in which the common people of any land ever declared themselves in favor of a gold standard. They can find where the holders of fixed investments have..."

..."Mr. Carlisle said in 1878 that this was a struggle between the idle holders of idle capital and the struggling masses who produce the wealth and pay the taxes of the country; and my friends, it is simply a question that we shall decide upon which side shall the Democratic party fight. Upon the side of the idle holders of idle capital, or upon the side of the struggling masses? That is the question that the party must answer first; and then it must be answered by each individual hereafter. The sympathies of the Democratic party, as described by the platform, are on the side of the struggling masses, who have ever been the foundation of the Democratic party. There are two ideas of government. There are those who believe that if you just legislate to make the well-to-do prosperous, that their prosperity will leak through on those below. The Democratic idea has been that if you legislate to make the masses prosperous their prosperity will find its way up and through every class that rests upon it..."

..."You come to us and tell us that the great cities are in favor of the gold standard. I tell you that the great cities rest upon these broad and fertile prairies. Burn down your cities and leave your farms, and your cities will spring up again as if by magic. But destroy our farms and the grass will grow in the streets of every city in the country. My friends, we shall declare that this nation is able to legislate for its own people on every question without waiting for the aid or consent of any other nation on Earth, and upon that issue we expect to carry every single state in the union..."

..."I shall not slander the fair state of Massachusetts nor the state of New York by saying that when citizens are confronted with the proposition, 'Is this nation able to attend to its own business?'-I will not slander either one by saying that the people of those States will declare our helpless impotency as a nation to attend to our own business. It is the issue of 1776 over again. Our ancestors, when but three million, had the courage to declare their political independence of every other nation upon Earth. Shall we, their descendants, when we have grown to seventy million, declare that we are less independent than our forefathers? No, my friends, it will never be the judgment of this people. Therefore, we care not upon what lines the battle is fought. If they say bimetallism is good but we cannot have it till some nation helps us, we reply that, instead of having a gold standard because England has, we shall restore bimetallism, and then let England have bimetallism because the United States has..."

..."If they dare to come out in the open field and defend the gold standard as a good thing, we shall fight them to the uttermost, having behind us the producing masses of the nation and the world. Having behind us the commercial interests and the laboring interests and all the toiling masses, we shall answer their demands for a gold standard by saying to them, you shall not press down upon the brow of labor this crown of thorns. You shall not crucify mankind upon a Cross of Gold!"

Where are the Thomas Jeffersons and the Andrew Jacksons and the William Jennings Bryans of today? Who is willing to risk it all, including their life, to alleviate the suffering of every man, woman and child on this planet Earth? With the current worldwide financial crisis, along with the internet, William Jennings Bryan would be unbeatable if he were running for the presidency today.

Unfortunately Bryan lost to McKinley by a small margin. Before the election workers were told by businessmen and industrialists that if Bryan won all the plants would be closed and many jobs would be lost. If the internet was around during that time the result of the election would have been reversed. Fear helped win the election for McKinley. Bryan's defeat in 1896 was a major victory for the big bankers; by squeezing the life out of the money system, they effectively steered the election process to their ends.

Let us look at some of the words of the bankers pre-1896 elections to gain a feel for what was at stake. A bank memo in 1891 from the American Bankers Association to members: "On September 1, 1894, we will not renew our loans under any consideration. On September 1 we will demand our money. We will foreclose and become mortgagees in possession. We can take two-thirds of the farms west of the Mississippi and thousands of them east of the Mississippi as well, at our own price... Then the farmers will become tenants as in

England..."

And from Charles Lindbergh's 1913 book "Banking and Currency and the Money Trust" another bank memo: "Silver, silver certificates, and treasury bonds (all government created money) must be retired and (interest bearing) national bank notes made the only money. You will at once retire one-third of your circulation (your paper money) and call in one-half your loans. Be careful to make a monetary (emergency) among your patrons, especially among influential businessmen. The future of (our debt based money system) depends upon immediate action, as there is an increasing sentiment in favor of government legal-tender notes and silver coinage."

This is what Bryan was going up against. The effects of the bankers' actions resulted in the failure of 500 banks and 15,000 companies. As the banks/bankers owned most of the gold it was easy for them to create depressions. The panic of 1893 was a bank created depression with the unfortunate unemployment, foreclosures and human suffering. As the depression continued, bankers continued buying up the foreclosed farms at pennies on the dollar.

From 1892, United States Bankers magazine: "We must go forward cautiously and consolidate each acquired position, because already the inferior social stratum of society is giving increasing signs of agitation. Let us make use of the courts... When, through the law's intervention, the common people shall have lost their homes, they will be more easy to control and more easy to govern, and they shall not be able to resist the strong hand of the government acting in accordance with... The control of the leaders of finance... We must keep the people busy with practical antagonisms. We'll therefore speed up the question of reform (of tariffs) within the Democratic party; and we'll put the spotlight on the question of protection... (for) the republican party. By dividing the electorate this way, we'll be able to have them spend their energies at struggling among themselves on questions that, for us, have no importance whatsoever."

This was what Bryan was up against. Keep in mind there was a bank caused depression during Democratic President Grover Cleveland's 2nd term, 1893-1897. God only knows the manipulations of the economy which take place. Gas prices somehow seem to skyrocket in an election year. Oil profits increase dramatically while keeping the debate on anything but the most important issues of international finance. Prices rise for some unknown reason, etc. Thank God the manipulations are coming to an end.

After the panic of 1907 the bankers continued with their push for private, central bank control of the monetary system. They decried that "drastic reform is needed". A central bank would stop the commercial banks' cycle of boom and bust. The use of propaganda to convince Congress and the American people was begun as alliances were formed with the media, journalists, economists, intellectuals, historians and social scientists advocating for the central bank. In 1910 the secretive six man meeting at J.P. Morgan's Jekyll Island, Georgia resort took place for one week. The six men went on Morgan's private train under assumed names for a "duck hunting" trip. Rockefeller and Morgan planned the federal reserve act.

Democrats won the 1910 elections and the bill was held off for a vote until it was renamed from the republican Aldrich bill to the democrat Glass bill.

The year 1913 saw the landmark enactment of the federal reserve act, establishing the federal reserve banking system. At the time Minnesota republican Congressman Charles Lindbergh Sr. (1859-1924) was one the leading opponents of the act. He said during this time: "To cause high prices, all the federal reserve board will do will be to lower their discount rate... Producing an expansion of credit and a rising stock market, then when... Businessmen are adjusted to these conditions, it can check... Prosperity in mid-career by arbitrarily raising the rate of interest. It can cause the pendulum of a rising and falling market to swing gently back and forth by slight changes in the interest rate, or cause violent fluctuations by a greater rate variation and in either case it will possess inside information as to financial conditions and advance knowledge of the coming change, either up or down. This is the strangest, most dangerous advantage ever placed in the hands of a special privilege class by any government that ever existed. The system is private, conducted for the sole purpose of obtaining the greatest possible profits from the use of other people's money. They know in advance when to create panics to their advantage. They also know when to stop panics. Inflation and deflation work equally well for them when they control finance."

Congressman Lindbergh also said, "This (federal reserve act) establishes the most gigantic trust on Earth. When the President (Woodrow Wilson) signs this bill, the invisible government of the monetary power will be legalized... The worst legislative crime of the ages is perpetrated by this banking and currency bill."

The federal reserve act of 1913, despite objections like Congressman Lindbergh's, passed.

Woodrow Wilson signed the 1913 act into law. Wilson may have expressed regret here: "a great industrial nation is controlled by its system of credit. Our system of credit is concentrated. The growth of our nation, therefore, and all our activities, are in the hands of a few men... Chill and check and destroy genuine economic freedom..." and from another writing Wilson said: "We have not one or two or three, but many, established and formidable monopolies in the United States. ...We have come to be one of the worst ruled, one of the most completely controlled and dominated governments in the world. No longer a government by conviction and the vote of the majority, but a government by the opinion and duress of a small group of dominant men."

Perhaps Sigmund Freud had the explanation as to why Wilson would sign the federal reserve act into law. Sigmund Freud heard the statement attributed to Wilson after winning the election, "Remember that God ordained that I should be the next President of the United States. Neither you or any other mortal or mortals could have prevented this." Freud responded, "I do not know how to avoid the conclusion that a man who is capable of taking the illusions of religion so literally and is so sure of a special personal intimacy with the almighty is unfitted for relations with ordinary children of men."

Whatever the motivations of Woodrow Wilson, his signing of the federal reserve act of 1913 began the private banks' control over the money supply which, at this time, has lasted 99 years. So started the cycles of boom and bust that have continued to this day where we find between the years 2000-2008, the greatest bank swindle in history.

The problem is that the federal reserve is accountable to no-one. It has total control of the monetary system where everything is done in secret. In 1993 then finance committee chairman Henry Gonzalez called for full, detailed, independent audits of the fed along with videotaping of their meetings. At the same time Gonzalez called for the selection of the 12 regional bank Governors to be by the President as opposed to the banks in the regions. Bill Clinton opposed, saying: "...would undermine market confidence." How would market/public confidence be undermined? The federal reserve is an absolute oligarchy. Fed chair Greenspan said, "...that any changes would weaken the fed's ability to control inflation. The public needs absolute control by the fed to control inflation. ...makes it harder to control inflation if President appoints..."

Although the bankers call themselves the "fiercest of inflation hawks..." the truth is that they are the cause of inflation. The fractional reserve banking system increases the money supply through banks creating money out of thin air. Let us say that hometown bank has $10,000,000 in deposits, has a 10% reserve requirement, they then can loan $100,000,000. This is how money is created; as debt. Increase in the money supply causes inflation. Banks earn their profits from interest payments on loans, credit cards etc. So why would they want to slow inflation by lowering their lending?

Fractional reserve banking could almost be called counterfeiting. The original counterfeiters would gain the most as they are the first recipients. Then a decreasing gain to retailers, to a decreasing gain down the line, to the least gain for those at the end of the money line. Inflation hits the hardest on those with the least. Part of the blame is on speculators, wild spenders; part of the blame is on the central banks who are responsible for inflation and rising prices.

The fractional reserve system is fraudulent. All of society and the economies of the particular countries are harmed. Inflation results in devastating booms and busts. Everything economic is "great" as the boom/bubble expands. People see their 401k accounts and pensions increase. Then the inevitable bursting of the bubble and everything is not so great anymore. The banks call in loans, the money supply is contracted, credit is reduced and recessions are the result.

The present federal reserve system is nothing more than a financial cartel. Through history the financial elite have spent enormous sums to first gain control of the monetary system and second to keep that control. The interests of the federal reserve are not of the public, but for the financial interests of those involved in the financial industry and corporations. The fed has a monopoly on the issue of bank notes. It buys assets and prints legal tender.

Say it buys $1 billion in U.S. Government bonds from Goldman-Sachs. The fed writes a check for $1 billion to Goldman-Sachs and Goldman-Sachs deposits the check. Where did the fed's $1 billion come from? It was created out of thin air. $1 billion is added to the money supply, Goldman-Sachs' bank can now lend $10 billion out under the fractional reserve system. $11 billion, in this example, is added to the money supply. The fed is the so-called lender of last resort; it has the power to print money if the public demands cash from insolvent banks. If it buys assets the money supply increases; if it sells assets the money supply shrinks.

We cannot rely on the federal reserve to stop inflation; their actions always result in inflation along with ever more intense, damaging booms and busts. The federal reserve is in total control of the economy and it serves the rich elite. It can instigate recessions and depressions, thereby keeping unemployment levels up. Did anyone notice at the end of the George Bush term where Bush, Hank Paulson and Ben Bernanke were everywhere on the media more or less saying that unless Congress bailed out the banks the economy would collapse?

Those with only a minimum of economic knowledge would never have advertised such negative economic news to the entire world. We saw the results of that world-wide negative news with the choices of the people to slow their spending which made the economic conditions even worse. It makes you wonder if the advertising of the negative news was intentional.

Nationalize the federal reserve. Remove the power of the banks to create money by ending the fractional reserve system. Go to 100% reserve requirements. Money should be created by the government through infrastructure spending. Set up a monetary authority to monitor inflation by controlling the money supply. Increase the money supply through expenditures on health care, education and infrastructure improvements. Take the ability to control the quantity of the money supply away from private interests who only use that control to benefit private interests. There is no need for any type of gold or silver or any other metallic standard. Fiat money is not the problem; the real problem lies in the private creation of fiat money.

Banks will get their money/deposits as the government spends that money into circulation. The financial elite will oppose any effort to pass laws which restrict them in any way. They will oppose any type of regulations which prohibit them their freedom to commit frauds. They will say that if you do what the markets want you will be rewarded. If you do what the markets do not want you will suffer. Can anyone reading these words fail to observe where the present monetary system has led?

It has led to a worldwide economic disaster. Change is long overdue. The present financial system with its complex products such as credit default swaps, derivatives and the like is a predatory one. Those economists who defend this predatory system receive their paychecks from these same predators. Small, ineffective tweaks which fix nothing are what they suggest. The power of this predatory system, now in the hands of the predators that run it, must be taken away.

The United States of America has to reform its monetary policy now. The country's citizens deserve a system which has sound banking practices without the tremendous fraud and criminality at present. It is impossible to do a worse job with monetary policy than the private banks have done. People will say that the government taking control of the nation's money supply would be socialism. Talk to the members of the armed services, police and fire agencies along with teachers about socialism. These men and women provide essential services for our citizens. Those who would work at the government monetary office would provide essential services as well. They would not go into this work in order to make a killing and buy a jet and 10 vacation homes. They would be doing a valuable service to not only their country's citizens but the citizens of the world as well.

Those who cry socialism are using scare tactics in order to keep their monopoly power. Do not allow propaganda from the financial elites to stop you from seriously considering what is at stake here. The private banks bailouts to cover their frauds and gambling of epic proportions were given to those who engaged in massive criminality. This is fact. The top 25 banks on this planet have brought down the entire world. The stakes could not be higher. The citizens of other countries cannot believe how uninformed our citizens are. The American people must look and act on these issues with the same Spirit that those Americans in 1776 exhibited when they threw off the economic slavery of England.

Americans must gather the courage to demand no less than the passage of laws which establish a monetary reform which helps our citizens and humanity. Monetary reform is of the utmost importance; there is no more important issue facing humanity. Those who want to keep the present system will use psychological warfare by saying things like, "government is too corrupt..." and "nothing you can do will matter...".

The financial elites, the wealthy, are the cause of these problems. The present monetary system contains the evils of greed and lack of concern for humanity. The American people must face these evils and defeat them. It is long past the time that the American people and the rest of humanity are treated with decency.

The people of America and the world must become very informed and very active. Under the present monetary systems of the vast majority of the world's countries, all money is a pyramid of debt. These problems are political, societal and moral. All money that is created within the current monetary system is created as debt.

Inventor Thomas Edison (1847-1931) said in 1921, "if our nation can issue a dollar bond, it can issue a dollar bill. The element that makes the bond good, makes the bill good also. The difference between the bond and the bill is the bond lets money brokers collect twice the amount of the bond and an additional 20%, whereas the currency pays nobody but those who contribute directly in some useful way. It is absurd to say that our country can issue

$30 million in bonds and not make $30 million in currency. Both are promises to pay but one promise fattens the usurers and the other helps the people."

The revolutionary war was fought over the control of the issuance of money. The first Americans printed their own currency and the British could not stand for it. You do not read this, the real reason for the war of independence, in your history books. Government finances its debt by selling its government bonds for interest. If the government took over the control of the money supply eventually government debt would be a thing of the past. Debt-free money. Thomas Jefferson had eight straight years with a balanced budget. Later in American history the hero of the monetary reform advocates, Andrew Jackson, paid off the national debt.

The current national debt, if current monetary system is not abolished and replaced by government control of money supply, cannot ever be repaid. If the financial elites are allowed to remain in control of money then the economic life of America and the world will continue to be strangled. The financial elites have betrayed the entire population of the world. Ask yourself why we are having to borrow money from China and other nations. Ask yourself why the United States of America and most other countries of the world are suffering deep recessions, unemployment and unrest.

The rich get richer. The middle class suffers financial hardships. The poor get poorer. Assets are taken. The financial system has been exploiting for a long, long time. Look at the results and ask yourself if now is not the time to take care of these problems. The private banks' debt-money system has concentrated the wealth of the financial elites. The historical paradigm around money has unfortunately led to the unequal distribution of it to the detriment of humanity. The accumulation of money became, for those who possessed large amounts, a game to see who could accumulate the most. Studies have shown that, since the passage of the federal reserve act in 1913, the dollar has lost 95% of its value. The time to fix this inequity is right now.

During the savings and loan scandals of the 1980's there were around 1,500 convictions of those who committed fraud or other financial crimes. The economic crisis which culminated in 2008 was the result of financial fraud of a magnitude never before seen in human history. Words cannot adequately describe the unprecedented extent of the crimes. Simply, the frauds were epidemic. As opposed to the approximately 1,500 convictions of the 1980's savings and loan scandal there were virtually no convictions of those who committed fraud and other crimes during the economic crisis years of the late 2000's.

Documentary filmmaker Charles Ferguson's movie "Inside Job" won the Oscar for best documentary in 2011. The documentary is a powerful work which shows what really caused the 2008 economic crises and is one you will need to watch. Please do so as you will be astonished. As Ferguson accepted his Oscar the first thing he pointed out to billions of Oscar viewers was that, three years after the crisis, no executive had been arrested from the Wall Street firms that caused the crisis. Do you now see the power of these people? Bizarre. The lack of convictions, given the rampant fraud that occurred, is almost criminal. The government's justice department and the regulatory agencies with the power to enforce the laws of the land could be seen as accomplices.

In any area of endeavor the allowing of fraud with impunity results in a crisis. To continue the allowance of fraud with impunity will only result in another crisis... And another crisis. The crisis of the late 2000's destroyed tens of millions of jobs. The financial elites of Wall Street are weapons of mass destruction; mass destruction of jobs. During the savings and loan scandal of the 1980's the infamous Charles Keating brought Alan Greenspan to his aid to fix the problem. Greenspan became head of the federal reserve.

During the late 2000's scandal seventeen of America's largest banks left a trail of documentary evidence of fraud on massive scales. Many federal banks gave up their charters simply to become mortgage banks to escape the regulators. Everyone knew about the coming, disastrous economic time bomb that was on its way. The FBI warned Congress in 2004 that there was an epidemic of mortgage fraud which would result in an economic crisis. After the FBI warnings there was a massive increase in fraudulent mortgage loans. The lenders were the party that created so-called liars loans.

The largest banks in the world were actively involved in the creation of these millions of fraudulent mortgage loans. Then the loans were bundled into complex financial instruments, given AAA ratings by the ratings agencies and flushed down the toilet/sold to the next unfortunate owner of the toxic assets. To add insult to injury there is a way to bet that a stock will go down or that mortgages will not be paid. The same banks who bundled the toxic mortgages and sold them, knowing the customers would not be able to make the payments, bet large money that foreclosures would happen. It seems that transactions which "win" because of others' misery should be banned. Who invented the transaction where you can bet that a certain stock will decrease in value? Should not this type of transaction be banned as well, as it opens the way for all types of chicanery? The main point is that the selling of these toxic assets, known by the seller to be toxic, was the definition of insider trading. The fraudulent selling of assets.

Enron, before that house of cards fell, created the California energy crisis. Watch the 2005 documentary "Enron: The Smartest Guys in the Room" for the sordid story. There were regulations in the energy derivatives market and Enron took as much advantage of the absence of regulations as they possibly could for financial gain, in spite of the California citizens who paid through the nose for electricity. The documentary has audio of Enron employees laughing at the "suckers" in California. Now you know why those who champion de-regulation take that position. The less regulation, the more you can get away with. The more money. Period.

Please don't think that we are saying that all bankers are corrupt. Those who are honest would not commit frauds on the massive scale of those in the late 2000's scandal. The honest bankers would not use these complex financial instruments in order to deceptively sell toxic assets to others. Honest bankers would not make the bad loans as this would result in their bank's failure. They would not use appraisal fraud to increase illegally the values of the homes they finance. They would not make liars loans (false incomes) without any underwriting. Liars loans are not made by honest firms.

The epidemic of liars loans being made by most of the largest banks in America came to a point in 2006 where 1 out of 3 mortgage loans were liars loans. Approximately 2,000,000 liars loans were made in the year 2006. That is 2,000,000 fraudulent loans. Every mortgage lender in America was aware of the liars loan problem and yet the loans increased. Congress and the regulators knew of the warnings and the situation.

How can the financial elites be allowed to loot the system with impunity? During the savings and loan scandal of the 1980's between 500-700 financial elites were convicted of crimes. The late 2000's financial scandal resulted in 0 (zero) referrals, much less convictions of the much larger number of criminals compared to the S+L scandal of the 1980's. Estimates are that 10-12 trillion dollars were lost in the late 2000's scandal. If the wealthy elites, the 1%, are allowed to continue amassing wealth through worldwide fraud we will see crisis after crisis of increasing intensity and human suffering. This system of plunder is a direct assault on the American people and on the entire human race.

During the S+L scandal of the 1980's every member of Congress and every economist opposed re-regulation. The repeal of the Glass-Steagall act in 1999, originally passed in 1934 to prevent another depression, was de-regulation. It opened the door wide open for commercial banks to engage in activities and affiliations with securities firms, illegal under Glass-Steagall. Do not listen to those who cry de-regulation. These people and their companies absolutely must be very aggressively regulated. There must be very significant increases in the severity of penalties associated with financial crimes in order to deter future temptation. This means substantial prison time where, when those in the same area of commerce see the result of wrong choices and actions, the number of those crimes drops to a large degree.

In order to stop accounting control fraud by top bankers, very tough regulation, with the necessary manpower in white collar crime, is necessary. There is no alternative. Timothy Geithner was a total failure as a regulator when head of the New York reserve bank. Now he is the treasury secretary. The federal reserve had, and has, the authority to regulate every mortgage lender in the country. Alan Greenspan was anti-regulation and did nothing during the 2000's scandal. Ben Bernanke the same: Bernanke did nothing to stop the abuses and frauds. How are people who are against regulation chosen to be the top regulators? Attorney General Eric Holder and Treasury Secretary Geithner have been preventing any type of widespread prosecution of the huge numbers of fraudsters.

The federal housing finance administration found that 17 of the largest banks in the country made sales to the two most powerful housing entities, Fanny Mae and Freddie Mac, and left a paper trail which proved the banks made the sales intentionally while knowing they were fraudulent. Every form of justice is violated when the justice department refuses to undertake prosecutions. At this time the justice department is willing to give immunity while not even investigating for massive frauds in exchange for minor monetary penalties and fines. We see nothing less than the United States government's total surrender to crony capitalism.

Those who are in positions of authority whose job it is to regulate the financial markets and fail to do so must be replaced. Too big to fail firms must be made smaller so that their problems, associated with their systemic risks, do not become worldwide problems. All people everywhere should be outraged. Once again Alan Greenspan, Ben Bernanke and Timothy Geithner had the authority to stop the damage of the late 2000's economic crisis/scandal which spread worldwide. Those in power positions believe government regulation is the problem.

Crime pays at the largest financial institutions if nobody is prosecuted. The justice department has 20% of the number of FBI agents specializing in white collar crimes and prosecutors of white collar crimes than were available during the 1980's S+L scandal. The dollar amount of the late 2000's scandal was/is probably 50 times larger than the S+L scandal. White collar crime manpower should be increased to a point where it is larger than it was during the 1980's. Strong enforcement of regulations, re-regulation along with Glass-Steagall type laws should be passed to start putting an end to the rampant frauds and abuses in the financial industries. Shrink the size of the too big to fail companies so that their risks are minimized or eliminated.

One of the better news programs on television, "Frontline", had an episode titled "The Warning" broadcast in October of 2009. You can find the program on Youtube and you will be astonished after viewing it. The story documents the efforts of one woman who tried to warn the federal government in 1998 of the derivatives "time-bomb" but was pummeled because of her efforts, then ignored.

In 2005 there were economic cheerleaders everywhere. Things were booming in the economy with the housing bubble inflating steadily. A time of celebration. Alan Greenspan was awarded the Presidential Medal of Freedom by George W. Bush. Alan Greenspan, the "wizard" and Ayn Rand disciple who believed in the separation of the state and the economy. Federal reserve chairman beginning in 1987 and ending in 2006. A libertarian.

When Bill Clinton was elected President in 1992 there was a feeling in the country that government was the problem. Too much regulation by government was seen as a problem. Deregulation was seen as the answer by many at that time. Clinton appointed former Goldman-Sachs head Robert Rubin as treasury secretary. Greenspan and Rubin held similar views on Wall Street. They both believed that there should be less regulation of Wall Street firms. Timothy Geithner and Larry Summers, both also against "intrusive" regulations, were also on the Clinton economic team.

The market soared with the dot.com/internet bubble euphoria of the mid to late 1990's. These were economic boom times.

Brooksley Born was one of seven females in her years attending Stanford law school during the 1960's. She was the first female to become President of the Stanford law review and graduated at the top of her class in 1964. She had a long career in the legal field including in the areas of financial transactions and derivatives. Her name eventually came up as a possible choice for Attorney General under Bill Clinton but the post went to Janet Reno. She was offered and accepted the post to head the Commodities Futures Trading Commission

(CFTC) in April 1994.

Brooksley Born was 55 years old when she accepted the CFTC position in 1994. Ms. Born had seen in her legal career the worst of the markets and knew the importance of regulation. She had lunch with Alan Greenspan and was taken aback when Greenspan said, "the market will take care of fraud." In her job, she and her team found one area which caught their attention. That area was the over-the-counter derivatives transactions. These were transactions called swaps and were unregulated and had no transparency. They are traded over-the-counter by banks, insurance companies or other funds and companies. They were unregulated, big, growing rapidly and were out of sight. They are a form of gambling, bets. $27 trillion worth and growing dramatically.

Investigators for the CFTC eventually learned that the transactions were of a type that fraud was highly possible. In 1993 Bankers Trust sold derivatives to Proctor and Gamble which resulted in Proctor and Gamble suing Bankers Trust for fraud. Secret recordings of people at Bankers Trust included wording by their employees to the effect that "we are going to clean their clocks (Proctor and Gamble)." CFTC learned of the possible problems associated with these financial instruments after Proctor and Gamble and others sued Bankers Trust.

There was no record keeping, no reporting, no idea how big, trillions of dollars in transactions were secret and the market was growing rapidly. Born and her team put together a concept release to initiate regulation of over-the-counter derivatives/swaps. She had to get involved with Greenspan, Rubin and Larry Summers. At the time Greenspan was saying of the economy, "the economy is the best I have ever witnessed in 50 years..." When Brooksley Born told Larry Summers of her intention to start regulating over-the-counter derivatives, Summers read her the riot act. "You don't get it!" The banking industry begged to "get this lady off our backs!" Ms. Born found the reactions to her decision to regulate very suspicious. The President's working group, handpicked by Rubin, consisted of Rubin, SEC Chairman Arthur Levitt, fed chair Greenspan, Larry Summers and CFTC Chair Brooksley Born.

Born's concept release was to begin the process of regulating the derivatives market. Greenspan and Rubin were 100% against the regulating. "No, no, no. Deregulation has given us boom times."... "You do not have legal authority." Born replied that she did have the authority. Greenspan was angry, "this was serious mistake, unwise, tremendous damage..." "She's not playing ball, we will kill this." Born had her staff publish the concept release which landed her in the crosshairs of Greenspan, Rubin and Leavitt. They thought that

Congress must act to stop this. They began making Born to look like a power grabber.

Before Congressional committee Greenspan made the case against Born while she was pummeled by members of Congress, of which 90% knew nothing of derivatives; of their immense size and scope. In 1998 Born testified four times. She was up against very powerful forces and had no political capital, no support. Then Born's warnings became prophecy.

Trillion dollar hedge fund Longterm Capital Management was near collapse in 1998. LTCM used derivatives to leverage $5 billion into $1 trillion using a secret mathematical formula to create a "fool-proof" money machine. 44%, 40%, 29% returns... Then their computer models began failing. LTCM was doing transactions with fifteen of America's largest banks, was unregulated and investors could not evaluate LTCM's exposures. The Russian economic disaster at that time left LTCM close to collapse. The systemic risk of the collapse of LTCM was real and very scary. The entire economy was in jeopardy. After four days Wall Street banks bailed out the company/fund and the crisis passed.

This is what happens when there is no regulation of the gambling, Wall Street elites. Regulation of the o-t-c derivatives market was needed then and needed now. Greenspan at the time told Congress, "This was an anomaly... No new regulations... Regulation of the o-t-c derivatives market is quite adequate to maintain a degree of stability in the system..." O-t-c derivatives were left unregulated by Congress. Born was told there would be a regulatory freeze/prohibition on regulation of derivatives due to intense pressure exerted by the financial lobby and by Congress. Born resigned on June 1, 1999.

In 2007 the derivatives market grew to a mind boggling $595 trillion (yes, trillion). Estimates as of 2012 are $1,250 trillion. An unbelievable statistic. The time bomb explosion came in 2007, ten years after the collapse of Longterm Capital Management. On September 15, 2008 the collapse of Lehman Brothers made everyone aware of a financial crisis in both the U.S. and world capital markets.

Brooksley Born remained silent until 2009 when she said, "The market grew so enormously, with so little oversight and regulation, that it made the financial crisis much deeper and pervasive than it otherwise would have been."

SEC Chairman Arthur Leavitt changed his opinion of Brooksley Born, "I could have made a difference... I could have done much better."

The CFTC still lacks authority to regulate derivatives (as of October 2009 when the Frontline piece was produced). In a stunning testimony Alan Greenspan said to Congress after retiring: "Markets regulate themselves was a flaw. View was not right." Greenspan realized that his anti-regulation philosophy was flawed. Simply stunning.

With the abolition of the federal reserve the currency will be sound with no inflation. Remember Jesus and the moneychangers. This is a battle for humanity's freedom. The internet has played, and will continue to play, an essential role in the sharing of this important information by everyone on the planet. Do not allow any regulations proposed by governments to restrict in any way this tool called the internet. Consider why anyone would want to restrict the communication of ideas. Ideas are exactly what the human race needs at this time to come together and solve our problems. Do not take anything for granted. Do not be scared - fear will do no good at this time. Nothing but a change in consciousness is required now. When Jesus said, "What you do to the least among these, you do to me.", he was speaking truth. See all the suffering brothers and sisters on the planet right now. Grasp the real world situation and take strong, positive action to make the world situation better for all of our brothers and sisters everywhere.

A historical perspective is gained by reading the words of New York City Mayor John F. Hylan (1868-1936). John Hylan was Mayor of New York from 1918-1925 and he said in 1922, "The real menace of our republic is this invisible government which like a giant octopus sprawls its slimy length over city, state and nation. Like the octopus of real life, it operates under cover of a self created system... At the head of this octopus are the Rockefeller Standard Oil interests and a small group of powerful banking houses generally referred to as international bankers. The little coterie (n. An intimate and often exclusive group of persons with a unifying or common interest or purpose) of powerful international bankers virtually run the United States government for their own selfish purposes. They practically control both political parties, write political platforms, make catspaws of party leaders, use the leading men of private organizations and resort to every device to place in nomination for high public office only such candidates as will be amenable to the dictates of corrupt big business. These international bankers and Rockefeller-Standard Oil control the majority of newspapers and magazines in this country. They use the columns of these papers to club into submission or drive out of public office officials who refuse to do the bidding of the powerful corrupt cliques which compose the invisible government."

What has really changed since the days of John Hylan? Fortunately the means of communication, namely the internet, have allowed for a much larger dissemination of truth.

Unstoppable truth, thank God.

It is finally time for humanity to break the chains of the debt-money systems. Something is very wrong when we have as humanity all the abundance the Creator and Mother Earth has given us yet we have immense human suffering. When two friends have a few beers they describe what occurred as "We solved all the world's problems." Well the time has arrived where we as humanity will solve all the world's problems. The combined strengths, talents, ingenuity and efforts of the human race are more powerful than all the problems we face. The main ingredient of our success here on Earth is Love. With Love as the most important consideration when any action is taken, the future is unlimited.

Texas Congressman Wright Patman (1893-1976) sat on the house committee on banking and currency for 40 years, chairing the committee from 1965-75. In 1941 he said, "When our federal government, that has the exclusive power to create money, creates that money and then goes into the open market and borrows it and pays interest for the use of its own money, it occurs to me that that is going too far. I have never yet had anyone who could, through the use of logic and reason, justify the federal government borrowing the use of its own money... The constitution of the United States does not give the banks the power to create money. The constitution says that Congress shall have the power to create money, but now, under our system, we will sell bonds to commercial banks and obtain credit from those banks. I believe the time will come when people will demand that this be changed. I believe the time will come in this country when they will actually blame you and me and everyone else connected with this Congress for sitting idly by and permitting such an idiotic system to continue. I make that statement after years of study." Patman introduced legislation during twenty of his years in Congress to repeal the federal reserve act of 1913.

French economist Maurice Allais (1911-2010) said, "In fact, without any exaggeration, the current mechanism of money creation through credit is certainly the 'cancer' that's irretrievably eroding market economies of private property... In essence, the present creation of money, out of nothing by the banking system, is similar - I do not hesitate to say it in order to make people clearly realize what is at stake here - to the creation of money by counterfeiters, so rightly condemned by law." Needed is the end of fractional reserve banking and the beginning of 100% reserve requirements of lenders, along with the end of private central bank monetary control.

1976 Nobel Prize winner for economics Milton Friedman (1912-2006) had something to say about monetary policy, "The stock of money, prices and output was decidedly more unstable after the establishment of the (federal) reserve system than before. The most dramatic period of instability in output was, of course, the period between the two wars, which includes the severe (monetary) contractions of 1920-21, 1929-33 and 1937-38. No other 20 year period in American history contains as many as three such severe contractions. The evidence persuades me that at least a third of the price rise during and just after world war one is attributable to the establishment of the federal reserve system... And that the severity of each of the major contractions is directly attributable to acts of commission by the reserve authorities. Any system which gives so much power and so much discretion to a few men, (so) that mistakes-excusable or not-can have such far reaching effects, is a bad system..."

..."It is a bad system to believers in freedom just because it gives a few men such power without any effective check by the body politic-this is the key political argument against an independent central bank... To paraphrase Clemenceau, 'Money is much too serious a matter to be left to the central bankers.' ". Friedman also thought the great depression was caused by the federal reserve. Friedman said, "The federal reserve definitely caused the great depression by contracting the amount of money in circulation by one-third from 1929-33."

Two thirds of the planet is in debt. Countries that are in debt must seek investment in order to increase exports for debt repayment. John Perkins, mentioned elsewhere in these writings, was an economic hit man who enticed world leaders whose countries contained valuable resources coveted by trans-national corporations, to accept large loans from the World Bank and International Monetary Fund for infrastructure projects. This was a form of debt trap for the people of those countries. Those who stood up for their nation's independence and ownership of their natural resources many times were assassinated or overthrown by coups. This information must be understood by people to put an end to the practice and hold those responsible accountable for their crimes.

The leaders who took the loans and the financial elites of the country would get fabulously wealthy while the less fortunate must accept austerity measures to pay back the World Bank and IMF loans. This debt trap scenario practiced by international banks has been going on for too long. The people of each particular country are being robbed of their country's wealth and suffering lower standards of living in the process. The people of these countries do not want trans-national corporations in their land. They, just as all human beings, simply want to live a happy, healthy life. Think about why almost every country on Earth is in debt. It is this historical, wicked, economic game which is coming to an end.

As the economic crises has engulfed virtually the entire world there seems to be a call for a worldwide strategy for bringing solutions. How about a worldwide cable television station for the sharing of all the diverse economic opinions and options available for the human race to watch? Think outside the box. Why could not a project similar to this become a reality? At this point you will find channels on popular systems like "the knitting channel" or 100's of music channels. Perhaps a few of the redundant channels could be replaced by information channels dealing with the most important issues facing humanity. What is wrong with the people of the planet knowing what is happening that effects their lives? Just making the point here that those who own the major media in the world have a vested interest in not allowing real information getting to the populace.

We have in these writings given you some information that is uncomfortable as it deals with somewhat unpleasant, difficult issues. Keep in mind that all you need is to remain honest with yourself and others while rejecting anything having to do with greed and hate. We hope that you keep Love for others, your families and yourself as the guiding light when going on with your life. When more and more people allow Love to rule over every thought then we the people of Earth will be well on our way to establishing a fair, just world for all people.

President Franklin Roosevelt on the monetary fight, "The real truth of the matter is, as you and I know, that a financial element in the larger centers has owned the government ever since the days of Andrew Jackson-and I am not excepting the administration of Woodrow Wilson. The country is going through a repetition of Jackson's fight with the bank of the United States - only on a far bigger and broader basis." Once again thank God for the internet. Do not allow for any restrictions to be placed on this extraordinary means of communication for humanity.

We come across such information and we wonder how and why this situation came about. Our personal philosophies are examined. The inevitable confusion sets in about the whole set of reasons we have adopted to as we go through time. What are we doing with our lifetimes and why are we choosing what we choose? Are we hypnotically accepting society's ideals of what success and happiness are or are we exploring fully all of the different ways that men and women throughout history have attempted to explain the human condition? Or do we attempt to create original thought as a new way?

Since President Andrew Jackson gave his farewell address in 1837 the American people, along with humanity, have been swindled through the allowance of federal reserve/private corporation control of our money supply. If the private banks suffer financial losses, the taxpayer pays for the bailouts. The taxpayers absorb those losses. The private banks, when they realize profits, keep those profits.

The American people along with the people of the world must demand that the control of money be taken from private hands and placed in the hands of governments and the people. Time and again world history has shown us that private control of money leads to plutocracy or government by the wealthy.

The world's nations must all become the controllers of their currencies. This would eliminate all of the corruption, fraud and abuse practiced throughout history by private financial corporations. All the complex financial products, often used for fraudulent purposes, will be looked at, kept if a benefit for humanity, or banned if no benefits are realized for the people.

Countries around the world have the "minimum wage". What would happen if there were also a "maximum wage". This will be seen as really thinking outside the box. It is just a thought. It would be interesting to hear what the critics of such a proposal would use as arguments against. What human being could disagree that a "maximum wage" would result in a literal improvement in the living conditions of every man, woman and child on planet Earth? Since we have monetary systems virtually everywhere on Earth how about a "maximum wage" of $365,000 or $1,000,000 per year? It would seem that any human being should be able to live a fairly decent life anywhere on Earth with $365,000 or $1,000,000 per year. Perhaps a one year worldwide $365,000 or $1,000,000 maximum wage.

Imagine what kind of world we will live in when this "maximum wage" is signed into law. There will be enough resources to pay for the projects and actions which will eliminate many of the problems faced by humanity. Humanity has finally come to the point in history where there is no other choice but to solve our problems. Every action will result in the easing of our fellow brothers' and sisters' agonies and miseries. We will understand charity, compassion and Love.

We have been given overwhelming evidence, presented through history, of the financial and economic devastation brought about by those whose motivation is greed. We have all seen the banking scandals, Ponzi schemes, fraudulent derivatives, mortgage frauds, insurance scams, murders, sabotage, blackmail and right down the line of crimes committed because of the love of money. Now is the time to relegate greed to the history books. The banishment of greed will be seen by future generations as one of the most noble actions ever taken by mankind. Our children, grandchildren and great grandchildren will be eternally grateful to us for having created such a wonderful world for them.

The instituting of a "maximum wage" would go a long way towards eliminating corruption, fraud and deceit. After all, what is the motivation behind corruption, fraud and deceit where there are financial transactions? The motivation is to gain fraudulently at someone else's expense. Those who would object to the creation of a "maximum wage" argue that this move would reduce incentives for people to create and grow their businesses. They will argue that economic activity would be reduced as the incentives of the owners of business enterprises, actors, professional athletes, doctors, lawyers, hedge fund managers and anyone in the $365,000 or $1,000,000+ per year income range would be taken away.

Imagine the scenario where there is a $365,000 or $1,000,000 "maximum wage". First and foremost, the incentives which result in people using fraud and deceit to gain financially by stealing from others would be virtually eliminated. There would be a sharp decrease in financial crimes along with a sharp increase in the negative consequences felt by those who commit them. The historical concept of "making a killing" would no longer exist. All of the crimes committed in order to "make a killing", be they with the pen or the gun, would be reduced significantly.

The world's economic activity would no longer be based on making as much money as possible with sometimes economically devastating, malevolent acts of crime and fraud, but toward benevolent ends. More and more economic activity would be undertaken on the basis of goodwill, helping others and solving human problems. The dominant philosophy of "How much can I get?" will be replaced by the new dominant philosophy of "How much can I give?"

The major positive outcome of the institution of a "maximum wage" is that the incentives would change. The current incentive of profit maximization would be replaced by the incentive to help your fellow man. Those who would disagree with a $365,000 or $1,000,000 per year "maximum wage" would have to be asked the question: "Is your life all about you, or is it all about others?" This is the very basic Spiritual question which must be answered. This question goes into the very essence of the meaning of human existence. Here is the choice made between the ego and the Holy Spirit. Between Love and fear. There is no other choice.

Perhaps the maximum wage could be tested for just one year. Perhaps the rest of the countries on planet Earth would agree to the "One year for mankind and Mother Earth" implementation of the maximum wage. Imagine the profound increase/change in Spiritual awareness of the human race which will occur during this time. Can anyone debate that such a measure would not result in improvements over our current situation? What would be revealed about those who would object to a one year trial? Could their objection be, "How do you expect me to live on $365,000 or $1,000,000 a year?" Please know that this is a serious proposal.

Regulation of financial companies would be strictly enforced with appropriate punishments, including widespread public media attention given to those who take advantage of others through fraudulent gain. There will be no more monetary fines for illegal financial activities. The man who steals food to feed his family is given more real punishment than those who steal amounts thousands, millions, billions, even trillions of times larger.

Since 1913 the federal reserve banks of the United States and countries around the world with their manipulations of money supplies, markets and economies have caused booms and busts. Long term planning of business leaders has been stymied. The private federal reserve bank system is a failure. There have been eighteen recessions since 1913. Now the world depression of 2012. Nothing good comes from private control of money supplies. It is long past time for governments to take control of their money supplies.

As a result of the latest financial crises of 2008-2012 households in America have taken an eleven trillion dollar loss. What will it take to get serious action? Do not let "too big to fail" banks grow any larger, shrink them down to 50 billion dollars in assets over a five year period while intensively regulating them during the downsizing. Compensation systems are needed to eliminate incentives for the "big kill" on large, risky trades and transactions. At present there are tons of money in rewards if things go well, but possible destruction of global financial markets and losses in the trillions of dollars if the bets are lost. As of 2012 no serious re-regulation/Glass-Steagall legislation has been enacted. The Glass-Steagall act worked extremely well for sixty years and must be brought back now.

Austerity measures simply prolong and increase economic crises as less spending starts a vicious downward spiral. Government should be spending more and reducing taxes on the middle/lower income classes. Revenue sharing to states should be a large part of the spending to help states retain employees and provide essential services. Austerity in times of economic crises is insanity.

As of 2012 advanced industrialized countries, most notably Europe, are in depressions. Poor regulation and a hands off approach to the financial system has facilitated a prolonged recession and some think a depression. This is a situation that not many can remember. It is very serious. This is why the idea of a $365,000/$1,000,000 maximum wage was a serious proposal. The incomes of the top 1% have pulled away from the 99%; the top .1% has really pulled away to Gatsby-era levels of 1910. Income inequality has risen to 1930's levels. Part of the problem has been the difference of opinions of economists regarding policy directions.

Many have the erroneous opinion that the government should be like a household regarding finances. Government, especially during economic crises, must increase its role to intervene in the economy. Income inequality results in political inequality. Reforms in the political system are called for so that the 99% are fairly represented as opposed to the top 1% whose situations are very good. How much of the business that the financial sector does is for the enabling of productive, economic growth for the majority as opposed to actions which are concerned with individual gain and greed?

Banks have become market makers to take advantage of insider knowledge and tactics in order to maximize profits. Nobody is against making a profit but the balance between helping the country's economy/people and helping oneself has gotten way out of kilter. With so many homes under water the reduction of principals and interest rates should be undertaken to both stimulate the economy and help hard pressed citizens. The old paradigm of serving self is ending. The new paradigm of service to others is starting and unstoppable.

The cynicism and indifference of those who serve self with regard to the suffering people on the planet are being replaced by Love, compassion and an understanding that the problems which result in human suffering are solvable with relatively little resources. Those who have attained unbelievable riches are now being asked to share with those who are hurting. The historical inequality of wealth on Earth is being recognized as a Spiritual bankruptcy which has outlived itself. It is now time for the new dream.

Consider the economic examples given by Scandinavian countries like Finland, Norway, Sweden and Denmark. These peoples have high taxes but prevent politicians from lowering them as they experience solidarity, high academic achievement, low poverty, national healthcare and satisfactory living. The people in these countries have the highest standards of living on Earth and would not choose any other system than the one they have.

The tide has turned as the secrets can no longer be kept away from the people. The economies of individual countries and the whole world have been stolen by robber barons. Bankers have taken advantage of their customers with nothing short of thievery. Corporations run the government with men and women going into the government sector, back into the corporate sector, etc., etc. A few wealthy families benefit while the rest of the population suffers.

One half of the world's population lives below the poverty level. Many in America hold the belief that America has always been with its foreign aid an altruistic nation. It is not total altruism. The money/aid goes for the most part to American corporations and a few wealthy families in the recipient country. The supposed original intent of the aid to help the people of the recipient country is a fraud. You will not find any real investigative reporters on any of the major media to report these frauds. Laws are written by the 35,000 corporate lobbyists.

There are a small number of people on the planet who have one goal-the maximization of profits without regard to the consequences for the world's people and environment. These are the materialistic and greedy 1%. 60% of the world economy/budgets are spent on militaries for killing people. There are solutions available to create a better world. Thankfully these solutions are being shared by the people of the world through the worldwide web.

World consciousness and awareness are rising. Every person on Earth is facing the same economic crises, environmental degradation and climate chaos. It is a revolutionary time which is resulting in real human transformation. Leaders involved with greed, manipulation and brutality are being replaced by leaders whose leadership tools are Love, compassion and Peace. We the people are realizing that current leaders, especially those of the old paradigm, cannot be trusted to bring about the real changes needed to create the world that we the people want.

It is time to concentrate on positive and possible solutions to these obviously solvable human problems. Disinformation weapons are being beaten back with the new technologies of social media, the internet and smart-phones. Five corporations control the major media but these new technologies have overcome that control. We, the human race, will solve the poor's problems with increased help with farming, fishing and water issues - basic survival methods.

Enough spending on bombs, missiles, tanks and fighter jets. Time to end the desperate living conditions of our world's starving and poor. Let us begin by paying corporations to help the poor of the planet to grow their own food. Reject powerlessness and fear and the positive, possible changes we seek for humanity will become inevitable. There are so many solutions.

Private central banks in the form of the federal reserve of the United States. Worldwide banks in the form of the World Bank, International Monetary Fund and the Bank for International Settlements. There will be no more taking advantage of our fellow members of the human family for personal gain and self aggrandizement. That historical paradigm is over. Humanity has seen enough. The historical rule of ego thankfully is being eliminated. The new paradigm of the rule of Spirit is now thankfully being created.

Very few people control the money and wealth of the world. The suffering and misery experienced by our human family for hundreds of years has resulted in wealth going into the hands of these few. Now is the time for the reversal of this insidious human system. What we are talking about is basic fairness, justice and concern for our fellow man. What we are talking about is Jesus commandment, "Love one another as I have Loved you."

All of the suffering that humanity has experienced throughout history is finally going to be eliminated. War, hunger, poverty, disease, hate, greed, envy and misery are going be things of the past. Humanity is finally going to break the chains of egoic slavery and experience true Spiritual freedom. The human race is finally coming to the realization that we all are one. Imagine the glorious future that awaits us.

Get active with your actions being in harmony for humanity to win. When the people rise and make the changes necessary humanity will win. Believe a better world is possible and take the actions to make it happen. The human race created the money problems with their unfortunate consequences. The human race can fix these problems. Never doubt your ability to improve the situation in your country as well as your world. Never get discouraged and as the human race unites as one a better world will be created.

Future generations of humanity will point back to this time and know that this generation was the one. This generation was the one which took the actions necessary for the Creation of an everlasting Heaven on Earth. This generation was the one which understood the Spiritual philosophy of "seven generations". We are the generation which took the present and future into our own hands and created an everlasting Paradise on Earth. This generation will be remembered as the one where the awe-inspiring magnificent events took place. The events which changed everything for the betterment of humanity forever.

This generation will create the systems which distribute Mother Earth's abundance to all for the welfare of all. Not one single human being will be left out. There will be no more turning away from those who are struggling for survival. We have created the systems of inequality. Now the systems of equality will be created which will forever be understood as the best we could possibly create. Infinite Love will be the source of energy utilized in the Creation of these systems. Humanity will be happy to have created with infinite Love and reaching for our highest potential on Earth.

A utopia is defined as "An ideally perfect place, especially in its social, political and moral aspects". Why stop at utopia? A world created with infinite Love as its basis could not be described as anything but Heaven. The Creation of Heaven on Earth is what the physical realm/existence is all about. It is the reason we as souls come to the human, physical realm. Our evolution as immortal souls includes the realization of the truth of infinite Love and that awareness being communicated to all. When the awareness is possessed by all then the Creation of an infinite Love based physical reality begins.

We will know that we decided in favor of infinite Love because that was the only choice we could sanely make. All of our actions from that point will be based on only infinite Love. We will have reached the point in physical reality where beyond which it is impossible to go. Thy will, will be done, on Earth as it is in Heaven.

Many have come before this writer and many will come after who have and will speak on these things in a more articulate manner. Many of you have come across writings, music, film, speeches, art and other forms of communications that have profoundly moved you. We all are eternally grateful for the men and women who created these works. We simply pray that this effort results in positive consequences for those that come across it. We have attempted to be as honest as possible during this communication. Some will find the ideas shared as utopian, pie-in-the-sky or impossible. Perhaps the dream described is unrealistic but it is sincerely meant to be a benevolent dream. Perhaps humanity could go as far as is humanly possible. Perhaps that begs the question, "What is humanly possible?"

This generation will answer the question, "Is your life all about you, or is it all about others?" This generation will answer emphatically and collectively, "It is all about others." All will know that infinite Love is the only truth and that everything else is an illusion. We will understand that we are all forever beings and that nothing ever ends. With this level of Spiritual understanding all human activity will change to reflect that understanding.

Is this the truth of reality? We shall see. Humanity will find the way. Humanity will create a new world and it will be good. The people will dance and be happy. Welcome to the new world. Welcome to Heaven.

Part Two. The Spiritual Realm.

We will share with you here some passages from the Gnostic "Gospel of Thomas" writings found in Nag Hammadi, Egypt around 1945. After the excerpts from the "Gospel of Thomas" we will share writings from the "Secret Book of John". The Gnostic texts found were not included in the Bible that most of us are familiar with. There are certain passages which may give you further insights into the Spiritual world of Jesus that you were previously unaware of. We hope the passages give you comfort and strength. As some theories of life hold that all is Spirit/energy we have included this Spiritual information here for you. We hope that the writings add greatly to your Spiritual knowledge and awareness.

Here then are some passages from the "Gospel of Thomas".

"And he who shall find the interpretation of the words shall not taste death."

"And he who seeks, let him not cease seeking until he finds; and when he finds he will be troubled, and if he is troubled, he will be amazed, and he will reign over the all."

"If those who lead you say unto you: behold, the kingdom is in Heaven, then the birds of the Heaven will be before you. If they say unto you: it is in the sea, then the fish will be before you. But the kingdom is within you, and it is outside of you. When you know yourselves, then shall you be known, and you shall know you are the sons of the living father. But if ye do not know yourselves, then you are in poverty, and you are poverty."

His disciples asked him, and said unto him: "Wilt thou that we fast? And how shall we pray? Shall we give alms? And what rules shall we observe in eating?" Jesus said: "Do not lie; and that which you hate, do not do. For all things are revealed before Heaven. For there is nothing hidden which will not be manifest, and there is nothing covered which shall remain without being uncovered."

His disciples said: "Teach us concerning the place where thou art, for its necessary for us to seek after it." He said to them: "He that hath ears, let him hear. There is a light within a man of light, and it gives light to the whole world. If it does not give light, there is darkness."

"Love thy brother as thy soul; guard him as the pupil of thine eye."

"The mote which is in thy brother's eye, thou seest; but the beam which is in thine eye, thou seest not. When thou dost cast out the beam from thine own eye, then wilt thou see to cast out the mote from thy brother's eye."

"No prophet is acceptable in his village; a physician does not heal those who know him."

"A city that is built on a high mountain and fortified cannot fall, nor can it be hidden."

"What thou shalt hear in thine ear, proclaim to the other ear on your rooftops. For no man lights a lamp and sets it under a bushel, nor does he put it in a hidden place; but he sets it upon the lampstand, that all who come in and come out may see its light."

"If a blind man lead a blind man, both fall into a pit."

"The pharisees and the scribes have received the keys of the kingdom; they have hidden them. They did not go in, and those who wanted to go in they did not allow. But you be ye wise as serpents and innocent as doves."

"A vine was planted apart from the father, and since it is not established it will be pulled up by its roots and destroyed."

"They do not gather grapes from thorns, nor pluck figs from camel-thistles; they do not yield fruit. A righteous man brings forth a righteous thing from his treasure; a bad man brings forth evil things; for out of the abundance of his heart he brings forth evil things."

"If two makes Peace with one another in this house, they shall say to the mountain: be moved, and it shall be moved."

"Blessed are the solitary and the elect, for you shall find the kingdom; for you come forth thence, and shall go there again."

"If they say to you: whence have you come? Tell them: we have come from the light, the place where the light came into being through itself alone. It stood and it revealed itself in their image. If they say to you: who are you? Say: we are his sons, and we are the elect of the living father. If they ask you: what is the sign of the father in you?, tell them: it is a movement and a rest."

"Blessed are the poor, for yours is the kingdom of Heaven."

"He who has known the world has found a corpse, and he who has found a corpse, the world is not worthy of him."

"The kingdom of the father is like a man who had righteous seed. His enemy came by night, he sowed a weed among the righteous seed. The man did not allow them to pull up the weed. He said to them: lest perhaps you go to pull up the weed, and pull up the wheat with

96

it. For on the day of harvest the weeds will be manifest; they will be pulled up and burned."

"Blessed is the man who has suffered; he has found the life."

"Look upon the living one so long as you live, that you may not die and seek to see him, and be unable to see."

"Two shall rest upon a bed; one shall die, the other live."

"I tell my mysteries to those who are worthy of my mysteries. What thy right hand shall do, let not thy left hand know what it does."

"There was a rich man who had many possessions. He said: I will use my possessions that I may sow, reap and fill my barns with fruit, I may have need of nothing. These were his thoughts in his heart. And in that night he died. He that hath ears, let him hear."

"A righteous man had a vineyard. He gave it to husbandmen that they might work it, and he receive its fruit of their hand. He sent his servant that the husbandmen might give him the fruit of the vineyard. They seized his servant, they beat him, and all but killed him. The servant came and told his master. His master said: perhaps they did not know him. He sent another servant; the husbandmen beat the other also. Then the master sent his son. He said: perhaps they will reverence my son. Those husbandmen, since they knew that he was the heir of the vineyard, they seized him and killed him. He that hath ears, let him hear."

"Teach me concerning this stone which the builders rejected; it is the corner-stone."

"Blessed are you when they hate you, and persecute you, and do not find a place in the spot where they persecuted you."

"When you bring forth that in yourselves, that which you have will save you. If you do not have that in yourselves, that which you do not have in you will kill you."

"The harvest indeed is great, but the laborers are few; but pray to the father, that he send forth laborers into the harvest."

"There are many about the well, but nothing in the well."

"The kingdom is like a merchant who had a load of goods and found a pearl. That merchant was wise. He sold the load, and bought for himself the pearl alone. You also, seek after his treasure which does not perish but endures, where moth does not enter to devour, nor does worm destroy."

"I am the light that is over them all. I am the all; the all has come forth from me, and the all has attained unto me. Cleave a piece of wood, I am there. Raise up the stone, and ye will find me there."

"He who has known the world has found the body, and he who has found the body, the world is not worthy of him."

"Why do you wash the outside of the cup? Do you not understand that he who made the inside is also he who made the outside?"

"Come unto me, for easy is my yoke and my servitude is gentle, and you will find rest for your souls."

"Give not that which sets apart to the dogs, lest they cast them on the dung heap; cast not the pearls to the swine lest they grind it to bits."

"He who seeks shall find, and he who knocks to him it shall be opened."

"If you have money, do not lend at interest, but give to him from whom you will not receive it back." (Relates to the section on monetary reform)

"He who has found the world and become rich, let him deny the world."

"The Heavens shall be rolled up, and the Earth before your face, and he who lives in the living one shall neither see death nor fear; because I say: He who shall find himself, of him the world is not worthy."

The disciples asked: "On what day will the kingdom come?" Jesus said: "It cometh not with observation. They will not say: Lo, here! or; Lo, there! But the kingdom of the father is spread out upon the Earth, and men do not see it."

We hope that the passages from the "Gospel of Thomas" have added to your Spiritual knowledge and awareness. We will now share with you passages from the same group of Gnostic writings found in 1945 at Nag Hammadi, Egypt. This set of writings is called the "Secret Book of John". Here then are passages from the "Secret Book of John". Once again we hope that the reading of these passages gives you strength, comfort and adds to your spiritual knowledge of the world.

"I have come to teach you about what is, and what was, and what will be in order for you to understand the invisible world, and the world that is visible, and the immovable race of perfect humanity."

What is the realm we will be going to? Why did God send Jesus into this world? Or why did Jesus incarnate at this time? He told us, "This realm is modeled on the imperishable realm."

"All of a sudden, while I was contemplating these things, behold! The Heavens opened and the whole of Creation shone with a light from above."

"A little child appeared before me in the light. I continued looking at him as he became an old man. And then he changed again, becoming like a young man."

"I did not understand what I was seeing, but the one likeness had several forms in the light, and these likenesses appeared each through the other and the vision had three forms."

"He said to me, 'John, why doubt? Why be afraid? Don't you know this image?' "

"Be not afraid. I am with you always. I am the father, the Mother, the son. I am the incorruptible purity."

"I have come to teach you about what is, and what was and what will be. In order for you to understand the invisible world, and the visible world and the immovable race of perfect humanity."

"Raise your head; understand my lessons; share them with any others who have received the Spirit, who are from the immovable race of perfect humanity."

"The inexpressible one. The one rules all. Nothing has authority over it. It is the God. It is father of everything. Holy one, the invisible one over everything."

"It is uncontaminated, pure light no eye can bear to look within."

"The one is the invisible Spirit. It is not right to think of it as a God or as like God. It is more than just God."

"Nothing is above it. Nothing rules it. Since everything exists within it, it does not exist within anything. Since it is not dependent on anything, it is eternal."

"It is absolutely complete and so needs nothing. It is utterly perfect light."

"The one is without boundaries, nothing exists outside of it to border it. The one cannot be investigated, nothing exists apart from it to investigate it. The one cannot be measured, nothing exists external to it to measure it."

"The one cannot be seen, for no one can envision it. The one is eternal, for it exists forever. The one is inconceivable, for no one can comprehend it. The one is indescribable, for no one can put any words to it."

"The one is infinite light, purity, holiness, stainless."

"The one is incomprehensible, perfectly free from corruption. Not "perfect", not "blessed", not "divine", but superior to such concepts. Neither physical nor unphysical, neither immense nor infinitesimal. It is impossible to specify in quantity or quality, for it is beyond knowledge."

"The one is not a being among other beings. It is vastly superior, but it is not 'superior'."

"It is outside of realms of being and time, for whatever is within realms of being was created, and whatever is within time had time allotted to it. The one receives nothing from anything. It simply apprehends itself in its own perfect light."

"The one is majestic. The one is measureless majesty."

"Chief of all realms, producing all realms. Light producing light. Life producing life. Blessedness producing blessedness. Knowledge producing knowledge. Good producing goodness. Mercy producing mercy. Generous producing generosity."

"It gives forth light beyond measure, beyond comprehension."

"His realm is eternal, Peaceful, silent, resting, before everything. He is the head of every realm, sustaining each of them through goodness."

The Origin of Reality.

"We would know nothing of the ineffable and nothing of the immeasurable without the help of the one who comes forth from the one who is the father. He alone has informed us."

"The father is surrounded by light. He apprehends himself in that light which is the pure spring of the water of life that sustains all realms."

"He is conscious of his image everywhere around him, perceiving his image in this spring of Spirit pouring forth from himself. He is enamored of the image he sees in the light-water, the spring of pure light-water enveloping him."

"His self-aware thought came into being, appearing to him in the effulgence (brilliant radiance) of his light. She stood before him."

"This, then, is the first of the powers, prior to everything. Arising out of the mind of the father the providence of everything. Her light reflects his light."

"She is from his image in his light, perfect in power, image of the invisible, perfect virgin Spirit."

"She is the initial power, glory of Barbelo (the first emanation of the absolute), glorious among the realms, glory of revelation."

"She gave glory to the virgin Spirit, she praised him for she arose from him."

"She is the universal womb, she is before everything. She is: Mother-father, firstman, Holy Spirit, thrice male, thrice powerful, thrice named."

"Androgynous eternal realm first to arise among the invisible realms."

"She, Barbelo, asked the virgin Spirit for foreknowledge. The Spirit agreed. Foreknowledge came forth and stood by providence. Foreknowledge gave glory to the Spirit and to Barbelo, the Spirit's perfect power, for she was the reason it had come into being."

Primary Structures of the Divine Mind.

"She, Barbelo, asked the virgin Spirit for incorruptibility. The Spirit agreed. Incorruptibility came forth and stood by thought and foreknowledge."

"Incorruptibility gave glory to the invisible virgin Spirit and to Barbelo, for she was the reason that it had come into being."

"She asked for everlasting life. The Spirit agreed. Everlasting life came forth and they all stood together. They gave glory to the invisible Spirit, and to Barbelo, for she was the reason that it had come into being."

"She asked for truth. The Spirit agreed. Truth came forth and they all stood together. They gave glory to the invisible Spirit, and to Barbelo, for she was the reason that it had come into being."

"This is the five-fold realm of the father: the first man who is the image of the invisible Spirit, who is providence, who is Barbelo, who is thought. And foreknowledge-incorruptibility-life everlasting-truth."

Secondary Structures of the Divine Mind.

"The father looked into Barbelo. Barbelo conceived and bore a spark of light who had blessedness similar to, but not equal to, her blessedness who was the only child of that Mother-father, the only offspring, the only begotten child of the pure light, the father."

"The invisible virgin Spirit celebrated the light that had been produced, coming forth from the first power who is the providence Barbelo."

"The Spirit anointed him with goodness, making him perfect. He stood in the Spirit's presence and it was poured upon him. Having received this anointing from the Spirit he immediately glorified him and he glorified the perfect providence. Because of her he had come into being."

"He asked for mind to be a companion to him. The Spirit consented. When the invisible Spirit consented mind came into being. It stood by the anointed and glorified the Spirit and Barbelo."

"He wished to act through the word of the invisible Spirit, whose will became an action and appeared with mind, glorifying the light. And then word followed will into being. Everlasting life and will, mind, and foreknowledge stood together. They glorified the invisible Spirit and Barbelo. Because of her they had come into being."

Tertiary Structures of the Mind.

"The Holy Spirit brought his and Barbelo's divine Autogenes (original manifestation of the Christos) son to completion in order that he could stand before the great invisible virgin Spirit as the divine Autogenes Christ and honored him with a mighty voice."

"The invisible Spirit placed the divine Autogenes over everything. All authorities were subordinated to him. The truth within him let him learn everything."

"From the incorruptibility, through a gift of the Spirit the four lights (consideration, understanding, perception and grace) arising from the divine Autogenes stood before him."

"Grace exists within the realm of the light called Harmozel, the first angel. Along with Harmozel are grace, truth, form."

"The second light is called Oriel and it stands over the second realm. With Oriel are conceptualization, perception, memory."

"The third light is called Daveithai and it stands over the third realm. With Daveithai are understanding, Love, idea."

"The fourth light is called Eleleth and it stands over the fourth realm. With Eleleth are perfection, Peace, wisdom (Sophia)."

"These are the four lights standing before the divine Autogenes."

"Twelve realms stand before the son of the powerful, the Autogenes, the Christ, through the intention and the grace of the invisible Spirit. Twelve realms belong to the son of the Autogenes."

"From the perfect mind's foreknowledge through the intention of the invisible Spirit and the Autogenes' will, the perfect human appeared, its first true manifestation."

"The virgin Spirit named the human Adamas and placed him over the first realm with the mighty Autogenes Christ. With the first light Harmozel and its power, the invisible one gave Adamas invincible power of mind."

"Adamas spoke, glorifying and praising the invisible Spirit: 'everything has come into being from you, everything will return to you. I will praise you and glorify you and the Autogenes and the triple realm: father-Mother-son, the perfect power.' ".

"Over the second realm was appointed Adamas' son Seth with the second light Oriel."

"In the third realm were placed the children of Seth with the third light Daveithai."

"In the fourth realm were placed the souls of those ignorant of the fullness, those who did not repent at once but who, after some time, eventually repented. They are with the fourth light Eleleth. All of these created beings glorify the invisible Spirit."

A Crisis That Became the World.

"It happened that the realm wisdom of conceptual thought, began to think for herself. She used the thinking and the foreknowledge of the invisible Spirit."

"She intended to reveal an image herself, to do so without the consent of the Spirit, who did not approve, without the assistance of her masculine counterpart, who did not approve."

"Without the invisible Spirit's consent, without the knowledge of her partner she brought it into being."

"Because she had unconquerable power her thought was not unproductive. Something imperfect came out of her, different in appearance from her. Because she had created it without her masculine counterpart she gave rise to a misshapen being unlike herself."

"Sophia (wisdom) saw what her desire produced. It changed into the form of a dragon with a lion's head and eyes flashing lightning bolts. She cast him from her, outside of the realms of the immortal beings so that they could not see him."

"Sophia surrounded him with a brilliant cloud, put a throne in the center part of the cloud so that no one could see it. She named him Yaldabaoth (God of the blind)."

"Yaldabaoth is the chief ruler. He took great power from his Mother, left her, and moved away from his birthplace. He assumed command, created realms for himself with a brilliant flame that continues to exist even now."

The Fashioning of This World.

"Yaldabaoth United with the thoughtlessness within him. He begot ruling authorities, modeling them on the incorruptible realms above."

"The first is Athoth. The second is Harmas. The third is Kalilaumbri. The fourth is Yabel. The fifth is Adonaiu. The sixth is Cain. The seventh is Abel. The eighth is Abrisene. The ninth is Yobel. The tenth is Armupiel. The eleventh is Melcheir-Adonein. The twelfth is Belias who rules over the very depth of Hades."

"He made the first seven rulers to reign in the seven spheres of Heaven. He made the next five rulers to reign in the five depths of the abyss."

"He shared a portion of his fire with them, but shared none of the power of light he had received from his Mother."

"He is ignorant darkness. When the light mingled into the darkness, the darkness shone. When darkness mixed with the light, the light diminished, no longer light nor darkness but dim."

"The dim ruler has three names: Yaldabaoth is the first. Saklas is the second. Samael is the third. He is blasphemous through his thoughtlessness. He said, 'I am God, and there is no God but me!' since he did not know where his own power originated."

"His rulers created seven rulers for themselves. Each of these authorities created six demons apiece, there came to be 365 demons altogether."

"Here are the seven authorities' names and physical forms: first, Athoth with a sheep's face. Second, Eloaios with a donkey's face. Third, Astaphaios with a hyena's face. Fourth, Yao with the face of a seven headed snake. Fifth, Sabaoth who has the face of a dragon. Sixth, Adonin whose face is that of a monkey. Seventh, Sabbataios with a face of flame and fire."

"These are the seven days of the week. These authorities rule the world."

"Yaldabaoth has many faces. More than all that have been listed so he can convey any face he wants to the seraphim around him."

"Yaldabaoth shared his fire with his seraphim but gave them none of his pure light, although he ruled them by virtue of the power and glory of the light he had received from his Mother." (he called himself "God")

"He United his thought's sevenfold powers with the authorities who accompanied him. He spoke and it happened."

"He named those sevenfold powers starting with the highest one. Goodness paired with the first: Athoth. Providence paired with the second: Eloaios. Divinity paired with the third: Astaphaios. Lordship paired with the fourth: Yao. Kingdom paired with the fifth: Sabaoth. Zeal paired with the sixth: Adonin. Understanding paired with the seventh: Sabbataios."

"Each has its own realm modeled on one of the higher realms. And each new name refers to a glory in the Heavens so that Yaldabaoth's demons might be destroyed."

"The demon's own names, given by Yaldabaoth, are mighty names but the powers' names reflecting the glory above will bring about the demons' destruction and remove their power. That is why each has two names."

"Yaldabaoth modeled his Creation on the pattern of the original realms above him so that it might be just like the indestructible realms."

"When he gazed upon his creation surrounding him he said to his host of demons, the ones who had come forth out of him: 'I am a jealous God and there is no God but me!' " (He admitted there was another God, as he was jealous)

"His Mother began to move back and forth because she had become aware that she now lacked light, for her brightness had dimmed."

"When she saw the evil that had taken place, and the theft of light that her son had committed, she repented."

"In the darkness of ignorance she began to forget. She began to be ashamed, but she could not yet return above. Yet she began to move, and so she moved back and forth."

"The arrogant one removed power from his Mother for he was ignorant; he thought no one existed except for his Mother. He saw the host of demons he had created and he elevated himself above them. But when the Mother realized that that miscarriage was so imperfect she came to realize that her consort had not approved. She repented and wept furiously."

"All of the divine realms heard her repentant prayer. They sought blessing for her from the invisible Spirit. The Spirit consented. He poured the Holy Spirit over her, brought forth from the whole full realm."

"She was elevated above her son, but she was not restored to her own original realm. She would remain in the ninth sphere until she was fully restored."

Humanity Begins.

"Then came a voice from the highest realms saying: 'The man exists! And the son of man!' "

"Yaldabaoth, chief ruler, heard it. He thought it came from his Mother, he did not know the true source of the voice: the Holy Mother-father, perfect providence, image of the invisible father of everything in whom everything has come to be."

"The first man. All of the realms of the chief ruler quaked! The foundations of the abyss moved!"

"He illuminated the waters above the world of matter, his image shown in those waters."

"All the demons and the first ruler together gazed up toward the underside of the newly shining waters. Through that light they saw the image in the waters."

"Yaldabaoth said to his subordinate demons: 'Let us create a man according to the image of God and our own likeness so that his image will illuminate us.' "

"Each one through another's power created aspects of the man; each added a characteristic corresponding to the psychic factors they had seen in the image above them. They made a creature of substance in the likeness of that perfect first man and they said, 'Let us call him Adam, so that his name will give us the power of light.' "

106

Construction of the Human Body.

"The seven powers began to work. Goodness made a psyche of bone. Providence made a psyche of sinew. Divinity made a psyche of flesh. Lordship made a psyche of marrow. Kingdom made a psyche of blood. Zeal made a psyche of skin. Understanding made a psyche of hair. The host of demons took these substances from the powers to create the limbs and the body itself."

"And those who were appointed over these parts are: Zathoth, Armas, Kalila, Iabel, Sabaoth, Cain, Abel."

"Seven govern the whole body: Michael, Ouriel, Asmenedas, Saphasatoel, Aarmouriam, Richram, Amiorps."

"There is a four-fold source of the bodily demons: hot, cold, dry, wet. Ruler of hot is Phloxopha. Ruler of cold is Oroorothos. Ruler of dry is Erimacho. Ruler of wet is Athuro."

"Their Mother stands among them: Onorthochraseai. She is unlimited, she mixes with all of them. She is matter and they are nourished by her."

"The four chief demons are: Ephememphi, associated with pleasure. Yoko, associated with desire. Nenentophni, associated with distress. Blaomen, associated with fear. The Mother is Esthesis-Zouch-Epi-Ptoe."

"Out of these four demons come passions: from distress arises envy, jealousy, grief, vexation, discord, cruelty, worry, mourning. From pleasure comes much evil and unmerited pride, and so forth. From desire comes anger, fury, bitterness, outrage, dissatisfaction and so forth. From fear emerges horror, flattery, suffering and shame."

"This is the total number of demons: 365. They work together to complete, part by part, the psychical and material body."

"There are even more of them in charge of other passions that I did not tell you about. If you want to know about them you will find the information in the book of Zoroaster."

"All of Yaldabaoth's servants and his demons worked to finish the psychic body. For a very long time it lay inanimate, it did not move."

"Yaldabaoth's Mother wanted to take back the powers she had turned over to the chief ruler. She earnestly asked the most merciful, the Mother-father of everything, for help."

Yaldabaoth Deceived.

"By his Sacred commands he sent down the five lights in the forms of the principal advisors to Yaldabaoth. They told Yaldabaoth: 'Blow some of your Spirit in the man's face, then his body will rise up.' Yaldabaoth blew some of his Spirit into the man. That Spirit was the divine power of his Mother."

"His Mother's divine power left Yaldabaoth, it entered the psychic human body modeled on the primordial image. The human body moved! It grew powerful! It shone!"

"Yaldabaoth's demonic forces envied the man. Through their united efforts he had come into being, they have given their power to him. His understanding was far greater than that of the chief ruler himself."

"When they realized that he shone with light and could think better than they could and was naked of evil, they took him and cast him down into the lowest depths of the material world."

The Beginning of Salvation.

"The blessed one. The Mother-father, the good merciful one, looked compassionately upon the Mother's power relinquished by the chief ruler."

"Since Yaldabaoth's demons might again overpower the perceptible psychic body, he sent down from his good Spirit a helper for Adam. Out of his great compassion a light-filled Epinoia (thought/idea) emerged, and he called her life."

"She aids the entire Creation working with him, restoring him to the fullness. She taught Adam about the way his people had descended. She taught Adam about the way he could ascend, which is the way he had descended."

"The light-filled Epinoia (thought/idea) was hidden in Adam, so that the rulers would not know about her. For Epinoia would repair the disaster their Mother had caused."

"The host of rulers and demons plotted together. They mixed fire and Earth and water together with four blazing winds. They melded them together in great turbulence. Adam was brought into the shadow of death."

"They intended to make him anew this time from Earth, water, fire, wind, which are matter, darkness, desire, the artificial Spirit. This all became a tomb, a new kind of body."

108

"Those thieves bound the man in it, enchained him in forgetfulness, made him subject to dying." (his was the first descent and the first separation)

Adam in Yaldabaoth's Paradise.

"The rulers took the man and put him into Paradise, they told him to eat freely. Their food is bitter; their beauty is corrupt. Their food is deceit; their trees are ungodliness. Their fruit is poison; their promise is death."

"They placed the tree of their life into the middle of Paradise. I will teach you the secret of their life: the plan that they made together about an artificial Spirit."

"Its root is bitter, its branches are dead. Its shadow is hatred, its leaves are deception, the nectar of wickedness is in its blossoms. Its fruit is death, its seed is desire, its flowers in the darkness. Those who eat from it are denizens (inhabitants) of Hades, darkness is their resting place."

"As for the tree called 'the knowledge of good and evil' it is the Epinoia of the light. They commanded him not to eat from it, standing in front to conceal it for fear that he might look upwards to the fullness and know the nakedness of his indecency."

"I asked the Savior, 'Lord, is it not the serpent that caused Adam to eat?' He smiled and replied, 'The serpent caused them to eat in order to produce the wickedness of the desire to reproduce that would make Adam helpful to him.' "

"The chief ruler, Yaldabaoth, knew that because the light-filled Epinoia within Adam made his mental abilities greater than his own, Adam had been disobedient. In order to recover the power that he had put into Adam, Yaldabaoth made Adam completely forgetful."

"I asked the Savior, 'What is it to be completely forgetful?' he replied, 'It is not what Moses wrote in his first book: 'He caused Adam to fall into deep sleep' rather, Adam's perceptions were veiled and he became unconscious. As he (Yaldabaoth) said through his prophet: 'I will make their minds dull so that they do not see or understand.' "

Woman Comes Into Being.

"The light-filled Epinoia (thought/idea) hid deep within Adam. The chief ruler tried to remove her from his ribcage, but Epinoia cannot be captured. Although the darkness pursued her it did not capture her."

"The chief ruler did remove a portion of his power from Adam to create a person with a woman's form, modeled on the light-filled Epinoia that had been manifested to him. He placed the power removed from the man into the woman." (not what Moses said, "he took a rib and made the woman.")

"Adam saw the woman standing next to him. The light-filled Epinoia appeared to him, she raised up the veil that dulled his mind. He sobered up from the dark drunkenness and he recognized his own counterpart."

"He said, 'This is the bone from my bones, flesh from my flesh.' Because of this man will leave his mother and father and be joined to a woman and those two will become one flesh. For they will send his helper to him."

"Sophia (wisdom), our sister, came down descending innocently so as to regain what she had lost. Therefore she was called life. The Mother of the living, the one from the providence of the authority of Heaven. By her assistance people can achieve perfect knowledge."

"I appeared as an eagle perched on the tree of knowledge! In order to teach them and raise them up from sleep's death."

"When Yaldabaoth discovered that they had moved away from him he cursed his Earth. He located the woman as she was preparing herself for her man. He gave the woman over so that the man might be her master, because he did not know the secret of the divine strategy."

"The man and the woman were too terrified to renounce Yaldabaoth, who showed his ignorance to his angels. And he cast both of them out of Paradise dressing them in heavy darkness."

"The chief archon saw the young woman who was standing by Adam. He realized that the light-filled Epinoia of life was within her. Yaldabaoth became completely ignorant."

"Yaldabaoth raped Eve. She bore two sons. Elohim was the name of the first. Yahweh was the name of the second. Elohim has a bear's face. Yahweh has a cat's face. One is righteous; one is not. Yahweh is righteous; Elohim is not. Yahweh would command fire and wind, Elohim would command water and Earth."

"Yaldabaoth deceptively named the two: Cain and Abel."

"Yaldabaoth installed the two with authority over natural elements so they can rule over the tomb."

The Children of Seth Populate the World.

"Adam had intercourse with the image of his foreknowledge, he begat a son like the son of man. And he called that son Seth, modeling him on the Heavenly race in the higher realms."

"In the same way the Mother sent down her Spirit, the image of herself, a model of the full higher realm, in order to prepare a place for the descent of the realms."

"The chief ruler, though, forced the humans to drink from waters of forgetfulness so that they might not know their true place of origin."

"The children (of Seth) remained in this condition for a while in order that when the Spirit descends from the Holy realms, the Spirit can raise up the children and heal them from all defects, and thus restore complete holiness to the fullness of God."

Six Questions About the Soul.

"I asked the Savior, 'Lord, will every soul be saved and enter the pure light?'

"He replied, 'You are asking an important question, one it will be impossible to answer for anyone who is not a member of the unmoved race. They are the people upon whom the Spirit of life will descend and the power will enable them to be saved and to become perfect and worthy of greatness. They expunge evil from themselves and they will care nothing for wickedness, wanting only that which is not corrupt. They will achieve freedom from rage, envy, jealousy, desire or craving."

"The physical body will negatively affect them. They wear it as they look forward to the time when they will meet up with those who will remove it. Those people deserve indestructible eternal life. They endure everything, bearing up under everything that happens so that they can deserve the good and inherit life eternal."

"Then I asked him, 'Lord, what about the souls who did not do these things even though the Spirit of life's power descended on them?' "

"He answered, 'If the Spirit descends to people they will be transformed and saved. The power descends on everyone and, without it, no one can even stand up. After they are born, if the Spirit of life increases in them, power comes to them and their souls are strengthened. Nothing then can lead them astray into wickedness. But if the artificial Spirit comes into

111

people, it leads them astray.' "

"Then I said, 'Lord, when souls come out of the flesh where do they go?' "

"He replied, smiling, 'If the soul is strong it has more of power than it has of the artificial Spirit and so it flees from wickedness. With the assistance of the incorruptible one that soul is saved and attains eternal rest.' "

"I then asked him, 'Lord, what of the souls of the people who do not know whose people they are? Where do they go?' "

"He responded, 'In those people the artificial Spirit has grown strong and they have gone astray. Their souls are burdened, drawn to wickedness, and cast into forgetfulness. When they come forth from the body, such a soul is given over to the powers created by the rulers, bound in chains, and cast into prison again. Around and around it goes until it manages to become free from forgetfulness through knowledge. And so, eventually, it becomes perfect and is saved.' "

"Then I asked, 'Lord, how does the soul shrink down so as to be able to enter its mother or a man?' "

"He was happy to be asked this and said, 'You are truly blessed because you have understood. The soul should be guided by another within whom is the Spirit of life. It will be saved by that means and accordingly will not have to enter the body again.' "

"And I said, 'Lord, what happens to the souls of people who achieved true knowledge, but who turned away from it?' "

"He said to me, 'Demons of poverty will take them to a place where there is no possibility of repentance. There they will stay until the time when those who blasphemed against the Spirit will be tortured and subjected to punishment forever.' "

"I asked, 'Lord, where did the artificial Spirit come from?' "

"And he told me:"...

Three Plots Against Humanity.

"The Mother-father is merciful, a Holy Spirit sympathetic with us. Through the Epinoia of the providence of the light it raises up the children of the perfect race, raising up their thought, their light eternal."

"When the chief archon learned that they were elevated above him and that their mental ability surpassed his, he wanted to put a stop to their thought, but he did not know the extent of their mental superiority, and he could not stop them."

"He made a plan with his demons who are his powers, each of them fornicated with wisdom (Sophia) and produced fate, the last variety of imprisonment."

"Fate challenges unpredictably. It is of different sorts, just as the demons are of different sorts. Fate is hard. Fate is stronger than the Gods, the authorities, the demons, the generations of people who are caught up in it."

"Out of fate emerged sinfulness, violence, blasphemy, forgetfulness, ignorance, weighty commandments, heavy sins, terrible fear. In this way all of Creation became blind, ignorant of God above everything."

"Because of imprisonment in forgetfulness they are unaware of their sins. They are bound into periods of time and seasons by fate who is lord of it all."

"Yaldabaoth eventually came to regret everything he had created. He decided to bring a great flood upon Creation, upon mankind."

"But the great light of providence warned Noah. He preached to all of the children, the sons of men. But if they were strangers to him they did not listen."

"Noah knew his own authority and that of the light being who illuminated them, although the chief ruler poured darkness over all the world."

"The chief ruler and his powers plotted a strategy, to send his demons to human daughters and make themselves children by them to enjoy. But they failed."

"After their failure they made another plan. They created an artificial Spirit modeled on the Spirit who descended so, to impregnate souls by means of the Spirit, the demons changed appearance to look like the women's husbands. They filled the women with that Spirit of darkness and wickedness."

"They brought into being gold and silver, money and coins, iron and other metals and all the things of this sort."

"And the people who were attracted were led astray into troubles and were greatly misled, and grew old experiencing no pleasure, and died finding no truth, never knowing the true

God."

"This is the way they enslaved all of Creation from the foundation of the world until now."

The Providence Hymn.

"I am the providence of everything. I became like my own children. I existed from the first. I walked down every possible road."

"I am the wealth of the light. I am the remembering of the fullness. I walked into the place of greatest darkness and on down. I entered the central part of the prison."

"The foundations of chaos quaked. I hid because of their evil. They did not recognize me. I came down a second time continuing on."

"I emerged from among those of light. I am the remembering of providence. I entered the middle of darkness, the inner part of the underworld, to pursue my mission."

"The foundations of chaos quaked, threatening to collapse upon all who were there and utterly destroy them. I soared upward again to my roots in light so as not to destroy them all yet. I descended a third time."

"I let my face light up, thinking of the end of their time. I entered their prison, the body is that prison. I cried out, 'Anyone who hears, rise up from your deep sleep!' "

"And the sleeping one awoke and wept, wiping bitter tears saying, 'Who calls me? Where has my hope come from as I lie in the depths of this prison?' "

"I am the providence of pure light," I replied, "I am the thought of the virgin Spirit raising you up to an honored place. Rise up! Remember what you have heard. Trace back your roots to me. The merciful one."

"Guard against the poverty demons. Guard against the chaos demons. Guard against all who would bind you. Awaken! Stay awake! Rise out of the depths of the underworld!"

"I raised him up. Sealed him with the light/water of the five seals. Death had no power over him ever again. I ascend again to the perfect realm. I completed everything and you have heard it."

Conclusion.

"I have told you everything now so that you can write it all down and share it with your fellow Spirits secretly. For this is the mystery of the unmoved race."

The Savior gave all of this to him to write and to keep carefully. He said to him, "Anyone who exchanges it for a present, or for food, or for drink, or for clothing, or for anything else of that sort will be cursed."

These things came to John in a mystery. Instantly the Savior vanished. John came to his fellow disciples and told them what the Savior had said to him. Jesus the Christ. Amen.

The Gnostic writings found in Nag Hammadi, Egypt include other books in addition to the ones we have seen here. There are a number of websites where you can do further study. We pray for your continuing Spiritual growth. Thank you.

A Course in Miracles.

In this section we are going to examine excerpts from the classic Spiritual work "A Course in Miracles". The material was scribed by New York psychologist Dr. Helen Schucman (1910-1981) between the years of 1965 and 1973. Dr. Schucman wrote the material in shorthand, receiving the messages from her "inner voice", some think Jesus Christ. The work is a three part Spiritual self-help course including the main text, a workbook and manual for teachers.

We believe you will find, no matter the source that these Spiritual messages are some of the most profound ever recorded. These excerpts are from chapter 27 through the 31st and final chapter of the textbook. Any comments will be enclosed as follows: (comments...). You will want to find the work for your own library as the information is of the kind where you will receive more every time you read it. There are websites available as well where you can read the entire work. Spiritual truth is found ahead in the words shared. We pray that your reading of these words will bless you, the entire human race and all of Creation.

All learning is a help or hindrance to Heaven. You but choose whether to go towards Heaven, or away to nowhere.

There is nothing else to choose.

Forgive the past and let it go, for it is gone. You have gone on, and reached the world that lies at Heaven's gate.

Look gently on each other, and behold the world in which perception of hate has been transformed into a world of Love.

God's answer is eternal, though it operates in time, where it is needed. But, because it is of God, the laws of time do not affect its workings.

It is in this world, but not a part of it. For it is real, and dwells where all reality must be.

Forgiveness is the only function here, and serves to bring the joy this world denies to every aspect of God's son where sin was thought to rule.

Forgiveness takes away what stands between your brother and yourself.

God wills you learn what always has been true, that he created you as part of him, and this must still be true because ideas leave not their source.

In every wish to hurt he chooses death, instead of what God wills for him.

To use the power God has given you as he would have it used is natural. The gift of God to you is limitless.

Let us unite in bringing blessing to the world of sin and death. For what can save one of us, can save us all.

There is no difference among the sons of God.

And yet to bless but one gives blessing to them all as one. Your ancient name belongs to everyone, as theirs to you.

Salvation is immediate.

Salvation would wipe out the space you see between you still, and let you instantly become as one.

And it is here you fear the loss would be, for a miracle is now. Be not content with future happiness.

The Holy Spirit's purpose now is yours. Should not his happiness be yours as well?

What has been blocked is opened; what was held apart from light is given up, that light may shine upon it, and leave no space or distance lingering between the light of Heaven and the world.

The holiest of all the spots on Earth is where an ancient hatred has become a present Love.

Your footprints lighten up the world, for where you walk forgiveness goes with you.

Where stood a cross stands now the risen Christ, and ancient scars are healed within his sight.

In gentle gratitude to God the father and the son return to what is theirs, and will forever be.

Now is the Holy Spirit's purpose done. For they have come! They have come at last!

Their presence is obscured by any veil which stands between their shining innocence and your awareness it is your own, and equally belongs to every living thing along with you.

God limits not. And what is limited cannot be Heaven, so it must be hell.

You have no enemy except yourself, and you are enemy indeed to him, because you do not know him as yourself.

The Holy Spirit's purpose is to let the presence of your Holy guests be known to you.

If you perceive injustice anywhere, you need but say, "By this do I deny the presence of the father and the son. And I would rather know of them than see injustice, which their presence shines away'"

Show this unto your brother, who will see that every scar is healed, and every tear is wiped away in laughter and Love.

And he will look on his forgiveness there, and with healed eyes will look beyond it, to the innocence that he beholds in you.

Forgiveness is not real unless it brings a healing to your brother and yourself.

Thus does the miracle undo all things the world attests can never be undone.

And hopelessness and death must disappear before the ancient clarion call of life.

The ancient calling of the father to his son, and of the son unto his own, will yet be the last trumpet that the world will ever hear.

Brother, there is no death.

And this you learn when you but wish to show your brother that you had no hurt of him. He thinks your blood is on his hands, and so he stands condemned.

But it is given you to show him, by your healing, that his guilt is but the fabric of a senseless dream.

In quietness are all things answered, and is every problem quietly resolved. In conflict there can be no answer and no resolution.

The only way to heal is to be healed. The miracle extends without your help, but you are needed that it can begin.

Accept the miracle of healing, and it will go forth because of what it is. It is its nature to extend itself the instant it is born.

The only thing that is required for a healing is lack of fear. There is no sadness, where a miracle has come to heal.

And nothing more than just one instant of your Love without attack is necessary, that all this occur.

Life is given you, to give the dying world.

The Holy instant's radiance will light your eyes, and give them sight to see beyond all suffering, and see Christ's face instead.

Thus is your healing everything the world requires, that it may be healed.

It needs one lesson that has been perfectly learned. And then, when you forget it, will the world remind you gently of what you have taught.

And happily your brother will perceive the many friends he thought were enemies.

Peace be to you whom is healing offered. And you will learn that Peace is given you, when you accept the healing for yourself.

What occurred within the instant which Love entered in without attack, will stay with you forever.

Yet all the witnesses that you behold will be far less than all there really are.

God thanks you for your healing, for he knows it is a gift of Love unto his son, and therefore is given to him.

As fear is witness unto death, so is the miracle the witness unto life. The miracle forgives because it stands for what is past forgiveness, and is true.

But there is need that you be healed, because the suffering of the world has made it deaf to its salvation and deliverance.

The resurrection of the world awaits your healing and your happiness, that you may demonstrate the healing of the world. What better function could you serve than this?

He cannot doubt his dreams' reality because he does not see the part he plays in making them, and making them seem real.

The choice is yours to make between a sleeping death and dreams of evil, or a happy wakening and joy of life.

Rest in the Holy Spirit, and allow his gentle dreams to take the place of those you dreamed in terror and in fear of death.

Dream your brother's kindnesses instead of dwelling in your dreams on his mistakes.

Let all your brother's gifts be seen in light of charity and kindness offered you. And let no pain disturb your dream of deep appreciation for his gifts to you.

The secret of salvation is but this: that you are doing this unto yourself. No matter what the form of attack, this still is true.

Whatever seems to be the cause of pain and suffering you feel, this is still true. For you would not react at all to figures in a dream you knew that you were dreaming.

Let them be as hateful and as vicious as they may, they could have no effect on you, unless you failed to recognize it is your dream. This single lesson will set you free from all suffering, whatever form it takes.

The Holy Spirit will repeat this one inclusive lesson of deliverance, until it has been learned, regardless of the form of suffering that brings you pain.

And you will understand that miracles reflect the simple statement, "I have done this thing, and it is this I will undo."

Remember nothing that you taught yourself, for you were badly taught. Who would keep a senseless lesson in his mind, when he can learn and can preserve a better one?

What you remember never was. The miracle reminds you of a cause forever present, perfectly untouched by time and interference. Never changed from what it is.

And you are its effects, as changeless and as perfect as itself.

The miracle comes quietly into the mind that stops an instant, and is still. It reaches gently from that quiet time, and the mind it healed in quiet then, to other minds to share its quietness.

And they will join in doing nothing to prevent its radiant extension back into the mind that caused all minds to be.

Born out of sharing, there can be no pause in time to cause the miracle delay in hastening to all unquiet minds, and bringing them an instant's stillness where the memory of God returns to them.

How instantly the memory of God arises in the mind that has no fear to keep the memory away.

The trumpets of eternity resound through the stillness, yet disturb it not.

What better way to close the gap between illusions and reality than to allow the memory of God to flow across it, making it a bridge an instant will suffice to reach beyond?

For God has closed it with himself. He has built the bridge, and it is he who will transport his son across it.

Have no fear that he will fail in what he wills. Nor that you be excluded from the will that is for you.

It is because he is God's son that he must also be a father, who creates as God created him.

The circle of Creation has no end. Its starting and its ending are the same.

But, in itself, it holds the universe of all Creation, without beginning and without an end.

The miracle does not awaken you, but merely shows you who the dreamer is. Do you wish for dreams of healing, or for dreams of death?

But, for this change in content of the dream, it must be realized that it is you who dreamed the dreaming that you do not like.

In dreams of murder and attack are you the victim, in a dying body slain.

But, in forgiving dreams is no-one asked to be the victim and the sufferer.

These are the happy dreams the miracle exchanges for your own.

It does not ask you make another; only that you see you made the one you would exchange for this.

The miracle establishes you dream a dream, and that its content is not true. This is a

121

crucial step in dealing with illusions.

No-one is afraid of them, when he perceives he made them up.

The fear was held in place because he did not see that he was author of the dream, and not a figure in the dream.

The miracle returns the cause of fear to you who made it.

The world is full of miracles. They are the dream's alternative, the choice to be the dreamer, rather than deny the active role in making up the dream.

The body is released, because the mind acknowledges, "This is not done to me, but I am doing this." and thus the mind is free to make another choice instead.

Beginning here, salvation will proceed to change the course of every step in the descent to separation, until all the steps have been retraced, the ladder gone, and all the dreaming of the world undone.

Healing is the effect of minds that join, as sickness comes from minds that separate.

Count, then, the silver miracles and golden dreams of happiness as all the treasures you would keep within the storehouse of the world.

The door is open, not to thieves, but to your starving brothers, who mistook for gold a shining pebble, and who stored away a heap of snow that shone like silver.

And what are you who live within the world, except a picture of the son of God in broken pieces, each concealed within a separate and uncertain bit of clay?

Be not afraid, but let your world be lit with miracles.

The door is open that all those may come who would no longer starve, and would enjoy the feast of plenty set before them there.

This is a feast unlike indeed to those the dreaming of the world has shown.

For here, the more that anyone receives, the more is left for all the rest to share. The guests have brought unlimited supply with them.

Here the lean years enter not, for time waits not upon this feast, which has no end.

For Love has set its table in the space that seemed to keep your guests apart from you.

There is a way of finding certainty right here and now.

Refuse to be part of fearful dreams whatever form they take.

Thus you separate the dreamer from the dream, and join with one, but let the other go.

It is his reality that is your brother, as is yours to him. Your mind and his are joined in brotherhood. Therefore release him, merely by your claim on brotherhood, and not on dreams of fear.

The Holy Spirit is in both your minds, and he is one, because there is no gap that separates his oneness from itself.

Your willingness to let illusions go is all the healer of God's son requires.

He will place the miracle of healing where the seeds of sickness were and there will be no loss, but only gain.

God is the alternate to fear. Where fear has gone, there Love must come, because there are but these alternatives.

Where one appears, the other disappears. And which you share becomes the only one you have. You have the one you accept, because it is the only one you want. There is no compromise. You are yourself or an illusion.

When you come to the place where the branch in the road is quite apparent, you cannot go ahead, you must go one way or the other.

It is only the first few steps along the right way that seem hard, because you have chosen, but you still think you can go back and make the other choice. This is not so.

A choice made with the power of Heaven to uphold it cannot be undone.

Your way is decided. There will be nothing you will not be told, if you acknowledge this.

The beautiful relationship you have with all your brothers is a part of you because it is a part of God himself.

Are you not sick if you deny yourself your wholeness and your health, the source of help, the call to healing and the call to heal?

Your Savior waits for healing, and the world waits with him. Nor are you apart from it.

For healing will be one, or not at all, its oneness being where the healing lies.

There is no middle ground, in any aspect of salvation. You accept it wholly, or accept it not. Either there is a gap between you and your brother, or you are as one.

(The house of faith, not faithlessness) the winds will blow upon it, and the rain will beat against it, but with no effect.

The world will wash away, and yet this house will stand forever, for its strength lies not within itself alone.

It is an ark of safety, resting on God's promise, that his son is safe forever in himself.

There is no time, no place, no state where God is absent. There is nothing to be feared.

Here is the fear of God most plainly seen. For Love is treacherous to those who fear, since fear and hate can never be apart.

No-one who hates but is afraid to Love, and therefore must be afraid of God. Certain it is he knows not what Love means.

He fears to Love and Loves to hate, and so he thinks that Love is fearful; hate is Love.

The fear of God! - The greatest obstacle that Peace must flow across has not yet gone. The rest are past, but this one still remains to block your path, and makes the way to light seem dark and fearful, perilous and bleak.

You had decided that your brother is your enemy. Sometimes a friend, perhaps, provided that your separate interests made your friendship possible a little while.

It is not Love that asks a sacrifice. But fear demands a sacrifice of Love, for in Love's presence fear cannot abide.

For hate to be maintained, Love must be feared, and only sometimes present; sometimes gone.

Thus is Love seen as treacherous, because it seems to come and go uncertainly, and offer no stability to you.

You do not see how limited and weak is your allegiance, and how frequently you have demanded that it go away, and leave you quietly alone in "Peace".

There is a shock that comes to those who learn their Savior is their enemy no more. There is a wariness that is aroused by learning that the body is not real.

And there are overtones of seeming fear around the happy message "God is Love". Yet all that happens when the gap is gone is Peace eternal. Nothing more than that, and nothing less.

Without the fear of God, what could induce you to abandon him? What trinkets or toys in the gap could serve to hold you back an instant from his Love?

Would you allow the body to say "no" to Heaven's calling, were you not afraid to find a loss of self in finding God? And can your self be lost by being found?

Why would you not perceive it as release from suffering to learn that you are free? Why would you not acclaim the truth instead of looking on it as an enemy?

Why does an easy path, so clearly marked it is impossible to lose the way, seem thorny, rough, and far too difficult for you to follow?

Is it not because you see it as the road to hell, instead of looking on it as a simple way, without a sacrifice or any loss, to find yourself in Heaven and in God?

Until you realize you give up nothing; until you understand there is no loss; you will have some regrets about the way that you have chosen.

And you will not see the many gains your choice has offered you. Why are you not rejoicing?

You are free of pain and sickness, misery and loss, and all effects of hatred and attack. No more is pain your friend and guilt your God, and you should welcome the effects of Love.

Whom you forgive is given power to forgive you your illusions. By your gift of freedom is it given unto you.

Make way for Love you did not create, but which you can extend. On Earth this means forgive your brother, that the darkness may be lifted from your mind.

When light has come to him through your forgiveness, he will not forget his Savior, leaving him unsaved. For it was in your face he saw the light he would keep beside him, as he walks through darkness to everlasting light.

This is the spark that shines within the dream; that you can help him waken, and be sure his waking eyes will rest upon you first, and in his glad salvation you are saved.

You cannot dream from some dreams and wake from some, for you are either sleeping or awake. And dreaming goes with only one of these.

For every dream is but a dream of fear, no matter what the form it seems to take. The fear is seen within, without, or both. Or it can be disguised in pleasant form.

The miracle were treacherous indeed if it allowed you still to be afraid, because you did not recognize the fear. You would not then be willing to awake, for which the miracle prepares the way.

Because he Loves the dreamer, not the dream, each dream becomes an offering of Love. For at its center is his Love for you, which lights whatever form it takes with Love.

There is a place in you where this whole world has been forgotten. Where no memory of sin and illusion linger still.

The changelessness of Heaven is in you, so deep within that nothing in this world but passes by, unnoticed and unseen.

The still infinity of endless Peace surrounds you gently in its soft embrace, so strong and quiet, tranquil in the might of its Creator, nothing can intrude upon the Sacred son of God within.

Nothing is asked of you but to accept the changeless and eternal that abide in him, for your identity is there.

Every thought of Love you offer him but brings you nearer to your wakening to Peace eternal and endless joy.

A dream is given you in which he (your brother) is your Savior, not your enemy in hate. Why does it seem so hard to share this dream?

Because, unless the Holy Spirit gives the dream its function, it was made for hate, and will continue in death's services.

Such is the core of fear in every dream that has been kept apart from him (the Holy Spirit) who sees a different function for the dream.

126

Forgiving dreams are means to step aside from dreaming of a world outside yourself. And leading finally beyond all dreams, unto the Peace of everlasting life.

You were not born to die. You cannot change, because your function has been fixed by God.

All other goals are set in time, and change that time might be preserved, excepting one. Forgiveness does not aim at keeping time, but at its ending, when it has no use.

Its purpose ended, it is gone. And where it once held seeming sway is now restored the function God established for his son in full awareness.

Time can set no end to its fulfillment, nor its changelessness. There is no death, because the living share the function their Creator gave to them.

Life's function cannot be to die. It must be life's extension, that it be forever and forever, without end.

This world will bind your feet and tie your hands and kill your body, only if you think that it was made to crucify God's son. For even though it was a dream of death, you need not let it stand for this to you. (Not crucifixion, but resurrection)

Let this be changed, and nothing in the world but must be changed as well. For nothing here but is defined as what you see it for.

How lovely is the world whose purpose is forgiveness of God's son! How free from fear, how filled with blessing and happiness!

And what a joyous thing it is to dwell a little while in such a happy place! Nor can it be forgot, in such a world, it is a little while until timelessness comes quietly to take the place of time.

Seek not outside yourself. For it will fail, and you will weep each time an idol falls.

Heaven cannot be found where it is not, and there can be no Peace excepting there.

There is no other answer you can substitute, and find the happiness his answer brings. Seek not outside yourself.

Be you glad that you are told where happiness abides, and seek no longer elsewhere. You will fail.

The fear of God is but the fear of loss of idols. Salvation thus appears to threaten life, and offer death. It is not so.

Salvation seeks to prove there is no death, and only life exists. The sacrifice of death is nothing lost.

An idol cannot take the place of God.

Let him remind you of his Love for you, and do not seek to drown his voice in chants of deep despair to idols of yourself. Seek not outside your father for your hope. For hope of happiness is not despair.

What is an idol? Do you think you know? Idols are but substitutes for your reality.

In some way you believe they will complete your little self, and let you walk in safety in a world perceived as dangerous, with forces massed against your confidence and Peace of mind.

This is the penalty for looking not within for certainty, and for a quiet calm which liberates you from the world, and lets you stand apart in quiet and in Peace unlimited.

This world of idols is a veil across the face of Christ, because its purpose is to separate your brother from yourself.

This is the anti-Christ; the strange idea there is a power past omnipotence, a place beyond the infinite, a time transcending the eternal. Here does the changeless change, the Peace of God, forever given to all living things, gives way to chaos.

And the son of God, as perfect, sinless, and as loving as his father, comes to hate a little while, to suffer pain, and finally to die.

Where is an idol? Nowhere! The world believes in idols. Each worshipper of idols harbors hope his special deities will give him more than other men possess.

It must be "more". It does not really matter more of what, - more beauty, more intelligence, more wealth; or even more affliction and more pain.

An idol is a means for getting more. And it is this that is against God's will. God gave you all there is.

And to be sure you could not lose it, did he also give the same to every living thing as well. No idol can establish you as more than God. But you will never be content with being less.

The slave of idols is a willing slave. For willing he must be, to let himself bow down in worship to what has no life, and seek for power in the powerless.

A dream of judgment came into the mind that God created perfect as himself. And in that dream was Heaven changed to hell, and God made enemy unto his son.

Whenever you feel fear in any form, - and you are fearful if you do not feel a deep content, a certainty of help, a calm assurance Heaven goes with you, - be sure you made an idol, and believe it will betray you.

Forgiving dreams remind you that you live in safety, and have not attacked yourself. Forgiving dreams are kind to everyone who figures in the dream. And so they bring the dreamer full release from dreams of fear.

The first rule, then, is not coercion, but a simple statement of a simple fact. You will not make decisions by yourself whatever you decide.

For they are made with idols or with God.

And you ask for help of Christ or anti-Christ, and which you chose will join with you, and tell you what to do.

Your day is not at random. There is no freedom from what must occur. And if you think there is, you must be wrong.

Decisions cause results because they are not made in isolation. They are made by you and your advisor, for yourself, and for the world as well.

Do you not understand that to oppose the Holy Spirit is to fight yourself? God but ensured that you would never lose your will, when he gave you his perfect answer.

Hear it now, that you may be reminded of his Love, and learn your will. He joins with you in willing you to be free.

And to oppose him is to make a choice against yourself, and choose to be bound. Look once again upon your enemy, the one you chose to hate instead of Love.

Now hear God speak to you through him (the Holy Spirit) who is his voice, and yours as well, reminding you that it is not your will to hate, and be a prisoner to fear, a slave to death, a little creature with a little life.

Your will is boundless; it is not your will to be bound. What lies in you has joined with God himself in all Creation's birth.

Remember him who has created you, and through your will created everything. God turns to you to ask the world be saved, for by your own salvation is it healed.

And no-one walks upon the Earth but must depend on your decision, that he learn death has no power over him because he shares your freedom, as he shares your will.

It is your will to heal him, and because you have decided with him, he is healed. And now God is forgiven, for you chose to look upon your brother as your friend.

The thought God holds of you is like a star, unchangeable in an eternal sky. So high in Heaven is it set that those outside of Heaven know not it is there.

But still and white and Lovely will it shine through all eternity.

Who knows the father knows this light, for he is the eternal sky which holds it safe, forever lifted up and anchored sure. But those who seek for idols cannot know this star is there.

Beyond all idols is the thought God holds of you. Surrounded by a stillness so complete no sound of battle comes remotely near.

It rests in certainty and perfect Peace. Here is your one reality kept safe, completely unaware of all the world that worships idols, and that knows not God.

You have not two realities, but one. An idol or the thought God holds of you is your reality.

Forget not, then, that idols must keep hidden what you are, not from the mind of God, but from your own. The star shines still; the sky has never changed.

But you, the Holy son of God himself, are unaware of your reality.

Reality observes the laws of God, and not the rules you set. It is his laws which guarantee you safety.

All illusions that you believe about yourself obey no laws. They seem to dance a little while, according to the rules you set for them.

But then they fall, and cannot rise again. They are but toys, my children. Do not grieve for them.

Appearances deceive because they are appearances, and not reality. Dwell not on them in any form. They but obscure reality.

And they bring fear because they hide the truth. God's son needs no defense against his dreams. His idols do not threaten him at all. His one mistake is that he thinks them real.

And you can make a simple choice that will forever place you far beyond deception. You need not concern yourself with how this will be done, for this you cannot understand.

But you will understand that mighty changes have been quickly brought about, when you decide one very simple thing; you do not want whatever you believe an idol gives.

For thus the son of God declares that he is free of idols. And thus is he free. No more than this is asked.

Be glad indeed salvation asks so little, not so much. It asks for nothing in reality. And even in illusions it but asks forgiveness be the substitute for fear.

Such is the only rule for happy dreams. The gap is emptied of the toys of fear, and then its unreality is plain. Dreams are for nothing. And the son of God can have no need of them.

They offer him no single thing that he could ever want. He is delivered from illusions by his will, and but restored to what he is. What could God's plan for his salvation be, except a means to give him to himself?

The real world is the state of mind in which the only purpose of the world is seen to be forgiveness.

The value of forgiveness is perceived, and takes the place of idols, which are sought no longer, for their "gifts" are not held dear.

Here it is thought that understanding is acquired by attack. There it is clear that by attack is understanding lost. The world becomes a place of hope, because its only purpose is to be a place where hope of happiness can be fulfilled.

And no-one stands outside this hope, because the world has been united in belief the purpose of the world is one which all must share, if hope be more than just a dream. Not yet is Heaven quite remembered. For the purpose of forgiveness still remains.

Yet he is glad to wait till every hand is joined, and every heart made ready to rise and go with him. For thus is he made ready for the step in which is all forgiveness left behind.

The final step is God's, because it is but God who could create a perfect son, and share his fatherhood with him. No-one outside of Heaven knows how this can be. For understanding this is Heaven itself.

And all that stood between your image of yourself and what you are, forgiveness washes joyfully away. The gap between your brother and yourself was never there.

Within your hand is everything you need to walk with perfect confidence away from fear forever. And to go straight on, and quickly reach the gate of Heaven itself.

For he whose hand you hold was waiting but for you to join him. An ancient hate is passing from the world, and with it goes all hatred and fear.

Look back no longer, for what lies ahead is all you ever wanted in your hearts. Give up the world! But not to sacrifice. You never wanted it.

What happiness have you sought here that did not bring you pain? Joy has no cost. It is your Sacred right, and what you pay for is not happiness.

Be merciful unto your brother, then. The will of God forever lies in those whose hands are joined. Until they joined, they thought he was their enemy.

But when they joined and shared a purpose, they were free to learn their will is one. And thus the will of God must reach to their awareness. Nor can they forget for long that it is but their own.

Anger is never justified. Attack has no foundation. It is here escape from fear begins, and will be made complete.

Here is the real world given in exchange for dreams of terror. For it is on this forgiveness rests, and is but natural.

Forgiveness recognized as merited will heal. It gives the miracle its strength to overlook illusions. This is how you learn that you must be forgiven too.

Look on your brother with the willingness to see him as he is. And do not keep a part of him outside your willingness that he be healed.

To heal is to make whole. Nor will you know him, if you think he does not merit the escape from guilt in all its forms and all its consequences. There is no way to think of him but this, if you would know the truth about yourself.

Appearances deceive but can be changed. Reality is changeless. It does not deceive at all.

And if you fail to see beyond appearances, you are deceived. The miracle is means to demonstrate that all appearances can change because they are appearances, and cannot have the changelessness reality entails.

The miracle attests salvation from appearances by showing they can change. What is temptation but a wish to make illusions real? There is no miracle you cannot have when you desire healing. But there is no miracle that can be given unless you want it.

The Christ in him is perfect. Is it this you would look upon? Then let there be no dreams about him that you would prefer to seeing this.

And you will see the Christ in him because you let him come to you. And when he has appeared to you, you will be certain you are like him, for he is the changeless in your brother and you.

Why should you fear to see the Christ in him? You but behold yourself in what you see. As he is healed are you made free of guilt, and his appearance is your own to you. Take heed then when you are called upon to fulfill your function as teachers that you teach the truth about God's son.

The only way that you can experience any Peace while this unfortunate necessity for interpreting illusions remains is to recognize that you are discussing only illusions, and that this has no real meaning at all. Try to say a prayer for your brother while doing this and you will call forth and experience a miracle instead.

How simple is salvation! All it says is what was never true is not true now, and never will be. Only unwillingness to learn it could make such an easy lesson difficult.

How hard is it to see that what is false cannot be true, and what is true cannot be false? Why, then, do you persist in learning not such simple things?

There is a reason. But confuse it not with difficulty in the simple things salvation asks you to learn.

It teaches you but the very obvious. The lessons you have taught yourselves have been so over-learned and fixed they rise like heavy curtains, to obscure the simple and the obvious.

Say not you cannot learn them. You who have taught yourselves the son of God is guilty, say not that you cannot learn the simple things salvation teaches you.

Yet you will learn them, for their learning is the only purpose for your learning skill the Holy Spirit sees in all the world. His simple lessons in forgiveness have a power mightier than yours, because they call from God and from yourself to you.

The certain outcome of the lesson that God's son is guilty is the world you see. It is a world of terror and despair.

The outcome of the lesson that God's son is guiltless is a world in which there is no fear, and everything is lit with hope, and sparkles with a gentle friendliness.

The soft, eternal calling of each part of God's Creation to the whole is heard throughout the world this second lesson brings. Without your answer is it left to die, as it is saved from death when you have heard its calling as the ancient call to life, and understood that it is but your own.

God's perfect son remembers his Creation. But in guilt he has forgotten what he really is.

Be innocent of judgment, unaware of any thoughts of evil or good that ever crossed your mind of anyone. Now do you know him not. But you are free to learn of him, and learn of him anew.

Now he is born again to you, and you are born again to him, without the past that sentenced him to die, and you with him. Now is he free to live, as you are free, because an ancient learning passed away, and left a place for truth to be reborn.

Let us review again what seems to stand between you and the truth of what you are. For there are steps in its relinquishment.

The first is a decision which you make. But afterwards, the truth is given you. Be very still for an instant.

Nothing will hurt you in this Holy place to which you come to listen silently, and learn the truth of what you really want. No more than this will you be asked to learn.

But as you hear it, you will understand you need but come away without the thoughts you did not want, and that were never true. He asks and you receive, for you have come with but one purpose; that you both may learn you Love each other with a brother's Love.

Together is your joint inheritance remembered and accepted by you both. Alone it is denied to both of you.

For next to you is one who holds the light before you, so that every step is made in certainty and sureness of the road. And he who travels with you has the light.

Learn this and learn it well, for it is here delay of happiness is shortened by a span of time you cannot realize. You never hate your brother for his "sins", but only for your own.

Are you sin? You answer "yes" whenever you attack, for by attack do you assert that you are guilty, and must give as you deserve.

Thus you think, within the narrow band from birth to death, a little time is given you to use for you alone; a time when everyone conflicts with you, but you can choose which road will lead you out of conflict, and away from difficulties which concern you not.

But they are your concern. How, then, can you escape from them by leaving them behind? What must go with you, you will take with you whatever road you chose to walk along. Real choice is no illusion.

But the world has none to offer. All its roads but lead to disappointment, nothingness and death. All of them will lead to death.

On some you may travel gaily for a while, before the bleakness enters. And on some the thorns are felt at once. The choice is not what will the ending be, but when it comes.

Men have died on seeing this, because they saw no way except the pathways offered by the world. And, learning they led nowhere, lost their hope.

And yet this was the time they could have learned their greatest lesson. All must reach this point, and go beyond it. The lesson has a purpose, and in this you come to understand what it is for.

Learn now, without despair, there is no hope of answers in the world. Think not that happiness is ever found by following a road away from it. A journey from yourself does not exist.

Where could it go? You cannot escape from what you are. For God is merciful, and did not let his son abandon him. For what he is be thankful, for in that is your escape from madness and from death. Nowhere but where he is can you be found. There is no path that does not lead to him.

You will make many concepts of the self as learning goes along. There will be some confusion every time there is a shift, but be you thankful that the learning of the world is loosening its grasp upon your mind.

And be you sure and happy in the confidence that it will go at last, and leave your mind at Peace. The role of the accuser will appear in many places and in many forms, and each will seem to be accusing you.

But have no fear it will not be undone. There will come a time when images have all gone by, and you will see you know not what you are.

There is no statement that the world is more afraid to hear than this: "I do not know the thing I am, and therefore do not know what I am doing, where I am, or how to look upon the world and on myself". Yet in this learning is salvation born. And what you are will tell you of itself.

You see the flesh or recognize the Spirit. There is no compromise of the two.

If one is real the other must be false, for what is real denies its opposite. There is no choice in vision but this one.

What you decide in this determines all you see, and think is real, and hold as true. On this choice does all your world depend, for here you have established what you are, as flesh or Spirit in your own belief.

If you choose flesh, you will never escape the body as your own reality for you have chosen that you want it so. But choose the Spirit, and all of Heaven bends to touch your eyes, and bless your Holy sight, that you may see the world of flesh no more except to heal and comfort and bless.

136

Salvation does not ask that you behold the Spirit and perceive the body not. It merely asks that this should be your choice.

It is your world salvation will undo, and let you see another world your eyes could never find. Be not concerned how this could ever be.

The veil of ignorance is drawn across the evil and the good, and must be passed that both may disappear, so that perception finds no hiding place. How is this done? It is not done at all.

What could there be within the universe that God created that must still be done? Only in arrogance could you conceive that you must make the way to Heaven plain. The means are given you by which to see the world that will replace the one you made.

Your will be done! In Heaven as on Earth this is forever true. It matters not where you believe you are, or what you think the truth about yourself must really be.

It makes no difference what you look upon, nor what you choose to feel or think or wish. For God himself hath said, "Thy will be done". And it is done to you accordingly.

One vision, clearly seen, that does not fit the picture as it was perceived before, will change the world for eyes that learn to see, because the concept of the self has changed.

Are you invulnerable? Then the world is harmless in your sight. Do you forgive? Then is the world forgiving, for you have forgiven its trespasses.

And so it looks on you with eyes that see as yours. Are you a body? So is all the world perceived as treacherous, and out to kill.

Are you a Spirit, deathless, and without the promise of corruption and the stain of sin upon you? So the world is seen as stable, fully worthy of your trust; a happy place to rest for a while, where nothing need be feared but only Loved.

Who is unwelcome to the kind in heart? And what could hurt the truly innocent? Thy will be done, you Holy child of God.

It does not matter if you think you are in Earth or Heaven. What your father wills for you can never change. The truth in you remains as radiant as a star, as pure as light, as innocent as Love itself. And you are worthy that your will be done.

Learning is change. Salvation does not seek to use a means as yet too alien to your

137

thinking to be helpful, nor to make the kinds of change you could not recognize. You cannot give yourself your innocence, for you are too confused about yourself.

But should one brother dawn upon your sight as wholly worthy of forgiveness, then your concept of yourself is wholly changed. And as you gave your trust to what is "good" in him, you gave it to the "good" in you.

And this will be your concept of yourself, when you have reached the world beyond the sight your eyes alone can offer you to see. For you will not interpret what you see without the aid that God has given you.

And in his sight there is another world. Have faith in him who walks with you, so that your fearful concept of yourself may change.

And all this shift requires is that you be willing that this happy change occur. No more than this is asked.

Hold out your hand, that you may have the gift of kind forgiveness, which you offer one whose need for it is just the same as yours. And let your cruel concept of yourself be changed to one which brings the Peace of God.

All that is given you is for release; the sight, the vision and the inner guide all lead you out of hell with those you Love beside you, and the universe with them.

And to each one has he allowed the grace to be a Savior to the Holy ones especially entrusted to his care. And this he learns when first he looks upon one brother as he looks upon himself, and sees the mirror of himself in him.

And in this single vision does he see the face of Christ, and understands he looks on everyone as he beholds this one. For there is light where darkness was before, and now the veil is lifted from his sight.

What is temptation but the wish to stay in hell and misery? Who has learned to see his brother not as this has saved himself, and thus is he a Savior to the rest.

The Holy ones whom God has given each of you to save are everyone you meet or look upon, not knowing who they are; all those you saw an instant and forgot, and those you knew a long while since, and those you will yet meet, the unremembered and the not yet born.

For God has given you his son to save from every concept that he ever held. For holiness is seen through holy eyes that look upon the innocence within, and thus expect to see it everywhere. This is the Savior's vision; that he sees his innocence in all he looks upon, and sees his own salvation everywhere.

For vision can but represent a wish, because it has no power to create. Yet it can look with Love or look with hate, depending only on the simple choice of whether you would join with what you see, or keep yourself apart and separate.

Be vigilant against temptation, then, remembering that it is but a wish, insane and meaningless, to make yourself a thing which you are not.

It is a thing of madness, pain and death; a thing of treachery and black despair, of failing dreams and no remaining hope except to die, and end the dream of fear. This is temptation; nothing more than this.

Can this be difficult to choose against?

Be not deceived by what appears as many choices. There is hell or Heaven, and of these you choose but one.

Let not the world's light, given unto you, be hidden from the world. Their Savior stands, unknowing and unknown, beholding them with eyes unopened. And they cannot see until he looks on them with seeing eyes, and offers them forgiveness with his own.

Can you to whom God says, "release my son!' be tempted not to listen, when you learn that it is you for whom he asks release? And what but this is what this course would teach? And what but this is there for you to learn?

(The following excerpts come from the final chapter of the textbook, chapter 31, The Simplicity of Salvation.)

Temptation has one lesson it would teach, in all its forms, wherever it occurs. It would persuade the Holy son of God he is a body, born in what must die, unable to escape its frailty, and bound by what it orders him to feel.

Would you be this, if Christ appeared to you in all his glory, asking you but this, "Choose once again if you would take your place among the Saviors of the world, or would remain in hell, and behold your brothers there". For he has come, and he is asking this.

How do you make the choice? How easily is this explained! You always choose between your weakness and the strength of Christ in you. And what you choose is what you think is real.

Trials are but lessons which you failed to learn presented once again, so where you made faulty choice before you now can make a better one, and thus escape all pain which what you chose before has brought to you.

In every difficulty, all distress, and each perplexity you face, Christ calls to you, and gently says, "My brother, choose again." he would remove all misery from you whom God created altars unto joy.

He would not leave you comfortless, alone in dreams of hell, but would release your minds from everything that hides his face from you. His holiness is yours because he is the only power that is real in you.

His strength is yours because he is the self that God created as his only son. The images you make cannot prevail against what God himself would have you be.

The Saviors of the world, who see like him, are merely those who choose his strength instead of their own weakness seen apart from him. They will redeem the world, for they are joined to all the power of the will of God.

And what they will is only what he wills. Learn, then, the happy habit of response to all temptation to perceive yourself as weak and miserable with these words: "I am as God created me. His son can suffer nothing. And I am his son."

You are as God created you, and so is every living thing you look upon, regardless of the images you see. What you behold as sickness and as pain, as weakness and as suffering and loss, is but temptation to perceive yourself defenseless and in hell.

Yield not to this, and you will see all pain in every form wherever it occurs but disappear as mists before the sun. Deny me not the little gift I ask, when in exchange I lay before your feet the Peace of God, and power to bring this Peace to everyone who wanders in the world, uncertain, lonely, and in constant fear.

For it is given you to join with him, and through the Christ in you unveil his eyes, and let him look upon the Christ in him.

My brothers in salvation, do not fail to hear my voice and listen to my words. I ask for nothing but your own release.

There is no place for hell within a world whose Loveliness can yet be so intense and so inclusive it is but a step from there to Heaven. To your tired eyes I bring a vision of a different world, so new and clean and fresh you will forget the pain and sorrow that you saw before.

But this is a vision which you must share with everyone you see. For otherwise you will behold it not. To give this gift is how you make it yours.

And God ordained, in loving kindness, that it be for you. Hear me, my brothers, hear and join with me. God has ordained I cannot call in vain.

And in his certainty I rest content. For you will hear, and you will choose again. And in this choice is everyone made free.

I thank you, father, for these Holy ones who are my brothers as they are your sons. My faith in them is yours. I am as sure that they will come to me as you are sure of what they are, and will forever be.

They will accept the gift I offer them because you gave it me on their behalf. And as I would but do your Holy will, so will they choose. And I give thanks for them.

Salvation's song will echo through the world with every choice they make. For we are one in purpose, and the end of hell is near.

In joyous welcome is my hand outstretched to every brother who looks with fixed determination toward the light that shines beyond in perfect constancy. Give me my own, for they belong to you.

And can you fail in what is but your will? I give you thanks for what my brothers are, and as each one elects to join with me, the song of thanks from Earth to Heaven grows from tiny, scattered threads of melody to one inclusive chorus from a world redeemed from hell, and giving thanks to you.

And now we say, "Amen": for Christ has come to dwell in the abode you set for him before time was, in calm eternity. The journey closes, ending at the place where it began.

No trace of it remains. Not one illusion is accorded faith, and not one spot of darkness still remains to hide the face of Christ from anyone.

Thy will is done, complete and perfectly, and all Creation recognizes you and knows you as the only source it has. Clear in your likeness does the light shine forth from everything that lives and moves in you.

For we have reached where all of us are one, and we are home where you would have us be.

(Author's note: that is the last of the excerpts from the textbook. Perhaps you will agree that the writings are some of the most profound ever written. We have not seen a work such as this where it seems that every word has meaning. Can you imagine the changes that will occur to all who read them? We are certain that the dissemination of "A Course in Miracles" will transform the world.)

(The following comes from the teachers manual / "Characteristics".)

And now in all your doings be you blessed. God turns to you for help to save the world. Teacher of God, his thanks we offer you, and all the world stands silent in the grace you bring from him. You are the son he loves, and it is given you to be the means through which his voice is heard around the world, to close all things of time; to end the sight of all things visible; and to undo all things that change. Through you is ushered in a world unseen, unheard, yet truly there. Holy are you, and in your light the world reflects your holiness, for you are not alone and friendless. I give thanks for you, and join your efforts on behalf of God, knowing they are on my behalf as well, and for all those who walk to God with me. Amen.

These writings are of the type that one gains more in every consecutive reading. What extremely powerful Spiritual passages. We think that you will agree and will read these passages again and again. Thank you.

Notes

The Near Death Experience.

There is much to be learned from the phenomena of near death experiences (NDE's). Perhaps there are some of you reading this who have experienced a "NDE". For those of you who have experienced a NDE some of this information will be very familiar, as you are well aware of the phenomena. Others of you reading this probably have had an out of body experience (OBE). OBE's are much more common than NDE's and are remarkable in their own right. OBE's are often called by other names such as astral projection or astral travel. Both NDE's and OBE's find a person leaving their physical body with their soul going on a Spiritual journey.

Perhaps some of you reading this have come across accounts told by those who have either had OBE's or NDE's. These stories are remarkable as they give us glimpses into the afterlife that are it seems important for all people to be aware of. Given the information we have been given about Spiritual truths the accounts of NDE's seem to set the record straight so to speak, on our ultimate reality. The increasing interest in the NDE phenomenon seems to be part of the waking up of humanity at this time. The descriptions given by people who have been to the "other side" are breath-taking and important.

There is no doubt that death is an illusion. Taking all the many thousands of NDE accounts from young and old, from all locations on Earth, we are left with no other conclusion but that there is no end to our existence. There are those who have tried to argue that the experiences are caused by hallucinations related to oxygen deprivation in the brain. There are other theories that try to explain the NDE's as other than the profound and real experiences for those who have had them. Any theory given which does not conclude that a NDE is a real separation of the person's Spirit from their body is wrong.

We will try to make the case that the NDE phenomenon are real and extremely important for humanity to become aware of. The information brought back by those who have had NDE's is of such magnitude that any and all measures must be taken to distribute the information to the ends of the Earth. You may go on your computer and type in "near death experience" and begin to be amazed when you find the personal accounts. The honesty of these accounts is obvious. Because the accounts are obviously honest we can only conclude the experiences are totally real. As they are totally real then the absolute importance of the experiences for humanity are again obvious.

The most compelling evidence for the reality of NDE's is seen when one realizes the great

144

similarities in content of them amongst young, old, varying nationalities, varying locations and varying pre-NDE Spiritual beliefs. There are common events seen in the thousands of recorded accounts that would seem to point to the inevitable conclusion that NDE's are real. The common features of the thousands of recorded accounts include travelling through a tunnel, seeing a bright light at the end of the tunnel, meeting relatives or friends who have passed on, seeing a review of one's life, being told "you have more to do" and not wanting to leave that place of profound beauty, Peace and Love.

We will examine the words used by those who have had NDE's and find that they are honestly shared. Many have not shared their accounts as they are afraid that others would think that they are crazy. Those who have shared their accounts were thankfully able to do so after they realized they were not alone. The subject of NDE's years ago reached popularity with the publishing of a number of books studying both the phenomena and personal accounts. Both researchers and NDEr's have been seen being interviewed on television and heard on radio interviews. There are now a number of websites devoted to the NDE where one can find personal accounts along with scientific studies.

The NDE phenomenon has become increasingly more well known as people find the descriptions given by those who have had them absolutely fascinating. When you find these accounts and read them you will also find them raising your consciousness. You will be thankful for finding these personal accounts as they will transform you. The truths contained in these personal NDE stories are truths which are of the utmost importance for humanity, all life and the living planet at this time. Thankfully the truths contained are becoming well known, as the dissemination of the Spiritual truths described in these accounts is raising the consciousness of more and more people on Earth.

We will get right to the personal accounts.

"I left my physical body. I floated to the ceiling and went through a tunnel at a high rate of speed. I was thinking faster and clearer. Felt the emotional states of oneness, Peace, joy. I entered an unearthly realm. I found myself standing beside my bed and was looking at me in the bed. Then I heard a voice saying, "Come with me". We went through a tunnel of light and on the other side everything was pure Love, pure Peace, pure perfection. I had the feeling that I was not worthy of such a place. I was given a life review which showed everything of my past. I felt the effects on others of every action I ever took when interacting with others... I felt what they felt at that time. I could see everything going on when I was outside my body... Nurses, doctors, outside the hospital, I saw my family members at home..."

145

Another account comes from a woman who had a blood clot at the brain stem/base of her brain. She recounts. "I popped out of the top of my head. I was looking down at the operation going on." What she saw while out of her body corresponded to what was occurring on the operating table. The conversations of the nurses and doctors corresponded to what they actually said. "I felt a presence. I saw a pinpoint of light and was pulled toward the light. I noticed figures, one of which was my grandmother. I went to her. I also saw an uncle who had passed and many people I knew. The light is God's breath. I was told it was time to go back but the more I was there the better I liked it. I did not want to go back into my body when my uncle told me to 'jump in'. My uncle pushed me back into my body." The doctors and nurses had no explanation for how she had seen and heard what she did.

Effects are extreme on those who have had a NDE. After returning to their bodies these men, women and children become less materialistic. They become less concerned about gaining status. They become more altruistic, they have an unselfish concern about the welfare of others. There are profound life changes seen in those who have had their experiences and return to their bodies.

Another man was involved heavily in the financial world. His sole purpose up to the point of his NDE was to accumulate money. He had a life threatening medical event and remembers, "Leaving my body and traveling to a place of profound, unconditional Love. The experience was beautiful, filled with purposefulness and overwhelming. Three Spiritual beings greeted me. I saw an old friend who I loved like a brother." He came to understand that his skills to make money had a purpose. At that moment his life changed. His heart became on fire with Love. He was a financial guru who severed all links with the business world. He became a counselor and is dedicated to improving the lives of others/helping others. "The mind is a separate entity that goes on after the body stops. I am thankful for the experience. Death is a lie and I am looking forward to it."

A woman suffered from a life threatening illness which resulted in her having excrutiating pain. "I prayed to be released from the pain. I found myself hovering near the ceiling. I followed a man through the ceiling and found myself in a new dimension. I was in a beautiful meadow and saw a city with streets paved with gold. I followed the man and saw my ancestors, family members and Heavenly figures. I spent time with the Savior as my younger self. There was an army of evil marching toward me as a child. I saw a light 5-6 feet away from my body which radiated pure, unconditional Love. The light said, 'Look to the light and live. What would you ask of me?' I gave Jesus my pain and felt his unconditional

Love. Bring your burdens to Christ and you will have the freedom of Peace."

A man suffered a heart attack at home. "I was watching my body from outside of my body. I now realize this is how everyone goes through it. I was watching the paramedics working on me. They took me from the house to the ambulance and I went through the wall of the house to follow them. I was behind the paramedic in the ambulance when I heard him say 'He's gone.' Then a tunnel formed and I was going through it. The tunnel was Peaceful, I felt safe and loved. It felt like I was going home. Heard chimes and then saw a bright, beautiful light. The light became a part of me and I became a part of the light. I saw a beautiful being who talked to me telepathically. I was then given a life review where I was there again experiencing every interaction with others that I ever had. I felt what the other person felt when I took the action. I felt their pain if I said or did something hurtful. Felt their joy if I did or said something loving. Nobody judged me, I was judging myself. I felt remorse, like a failure as a Spiritual being. I learned that we are responsible and we have to be the difference that God makes. This is how the Spirit can accomplish in the physical realm. I'm no longer afraid of dying so I'm no longer afraid of living."

We will all come to the point where our physical bodies will experience "death". Millions of people have had NDE's. There is a separation of consciousness where we will leave the physical body. The tunnels that people go through have a variety of different descriptions. So bright, brighter than the sun, it was all Love, took my breath away, the real world, home, tidal wave of unconditional Love. We will all have the life review where there will be no blame or judgment by anyone but we will judge ourselves.

A man was involved in a car accident and "died" at the scene. He describes what happened then. "It was like I was standing on a balcony looking down on the car with me in it. It was as if I was then sucked through a tunnel. I went through space and ended in an extremely bright, white light. It was totally loving and exuded profound Peace. There are no words which are adequate to describe that Love and Peace. Any questions that I had were answered in an instant. It seemed I was receiving more information than what you would find on the internet. Then Jesus looked directly into my heart as I watched my "life review". Then I was told that I had to go back."

Those who return from a NDE find it profoundly difficult to share because they are overloaded by the hurt and pain of the body compared to what they have seen and felt on the other side. The great majority of these people are changed. They no longer fear death and have found that they want to help others. They learn that we are all connected and they want to have nothing but a positive effect upon the world. They knew they were in Heaven and that everyone will have this experience. Some descriptions include: too amazing for words - profoundly comforted - pure, bright colors - never felt this happy - music too beautiful to describe - Love, joy, Peace - someone close by, intense Love - please don't send me back - not the same person - no way to describe the experience - no words - yes there is a Heaven.

One woman had a medical event and shares: "I found myself rising out of my body in a funnel shaped cloud. I was surrounded by a tranquil light and heard this stupendously beautiful singing. I came to a city which had a foundation of diamonds with solid pearl gates. I remembered Jesus saying 'In my father's house there are many mansions. Make me real to people on Earth.' Then Jesus came into my room and healed me. There was someone there to welcome me, to acclimate me. I saw the book of life and was told that we are always learning. Then I was told that my work was not finished and that I had to go back."

Another man was told, by a woman psychic friend, that he had lung cancer and was going to die. Being a veteran of Vietnam he was looked at by doctors at this V.A. Hospital who found the lung cancer. He would receive serious treatments after signing up for a clinical trial. One lung was removed and he had to undergo another serious operation after complications arose from the first surgery. He woke up from the surgery and was looking at the doctors in his room praying for his soul as they were sure he would die. The doctors noticed his eyes were open and blurted, "He's alive!" One doctor stayed while the others left the room. The doctor told him, "During the surgery you were talking to Jesus Christ."

The doctor added, "You were engaged in a two way conversation." The patient thought to himself that the doctor shouldn't be joking with him at that time, after such a difficult surgery.

The man went and saw his woman psychic friend. The moment she saw him, she froze. "You're all lit up with angels!" she was crying. "You're not supposed to be here. You left your body and screamed your regret at hurting anyone in your life. You told Jesus that you had lung cancer, you were getting government retirement checks and wanted to go back and have some fun. Jesus touched you and you were instantly healed. You will live another 25 years and you will help people, because that is all you want to do."

Another woman recounts an event she had as a child and an event she had as an adult. "There was a buzzing around my ears like I had been electrocuted. I was near the ceiling looking down at my body. As I moved toward this door I knew that if I went through the door I would not be coming back. I became aware of the universal consciousness that had every bit of knowledge that there ever was in the universe. I did not want to come back. I saw everything I had ever done, loving or unloving, to others."

As a child, "I met my grandparents, they told me I had a mission to complete on Earth. The guides would ask me, 'Don't you want to go back?' Nothing on Earth compares, you have never been so loved in all your life than during what they call death. I was looking at the surgeon from above. In the tunnel it was totally Peaceful, you don't have any language to describe it. The beings I met were completely compassionate."

A man shares his thoughts on what he learned from his NDE, "It seems to be important to touch the lives of others in a meaningful way. We should be surrendering to the moment as this moment is all we have. We should eliminate any fearful thoughts provided we live our lives following our calling and our passion. Nothing we strive for here like family, wealth, status, material possessions or power mean anything on the other side. The mistakes we make mean nothing on the other side. We are here to make mistakes to know that we are alive and to grow. The experience I had was definitely real. It has been the greatest gift of my life. I am truly blessed and grateful to have had this experience. I have changed my direction quite a few times since then and each move has expanded my life."

A woman describes "Being in a warm place. It was like I had an airline ticket and I was at the airport, waiting. The light exploded under me and went out in every direction. The light was infinite. There was nothing else to this light but Love. The experience was powerful and personal; the communication was through mathematics and music. I asked every question and the answers had nothing to do with learning, but remembering. I argued after being told that "You have to go back." then God through the math and music showed me a Kentucky-like Heaven where every blade of grass had consciousness, the colors were not like any on Earth. I was shown the future, people I would meet when I chose to go back. I learned my future would be about giving service."

Research has found ways to map out the process of dying to the point where we are on the verge of a huge transformation of thought about the afterlife. The interest in near death experiences is growing as people experiencing the aging process start asking "Is there something after this?" Those who have a NDE report that their consciousness is crystal clear, higher than when in the body. What these men, women and children saw and heard while out of the body has been proven to be 100% accurate so NDE's are beyond anything modern science can explain.

A man experienced a NDE while having open heart surgery. "I found myself in a dark void. Then I felt a presence, the presence coalesced into the light which contained the universe. There was nothing outside of it; I could not wrap my mind around the light. People and things which were important to me were attached by some type of cords; these cords dissolved one by one as I drew closer to the light. The light kept getting brighter to the point where I was at the edge of the light; I was merging with the light. My body was becoming the light, the infinite. It seemed like an hour was spent coming close to merging and then not merging; I realized that if I merged with the light that I would disappear into the unity. I would be leaving my body and dying. There would be no going back. Then I decided to go back. Now I try to be creative and totally present as much as possible."

Striking as well is that those met on the other side (relatives and friends) are always in picture perfect health. Of note as well is that the content of the NDE's from all around the planet are strikingly similar. Then you will find that the NDE's of small children are virtually the same as older children and adults. Small children have no knowledge of Spirituality much less near death experiences. This would have to be seen as dramatic proof of the reality of these experiences.

One man had two NDE's related to triple-bypass surgery. "The 1st time I remembered that death was so instantaneous that it was unbelievable. It is just a passage. A man came to meet me and he said, 'Follow me'. We went up through a "mud" tunnel and came into an incredibly bright room which had no climate. There were 250-300 people waiting there to greet me. They were thrilled to see me; every one of them hugged and kissed me. They were men and women who were radiant. They were exuding Love and beauty; I knew I was in Heaven/Paradise. I was led to sit on a table, while the 250-300 people were around, where I saw the movie of my life. As the scenes of my life went by one by one I noticed Jesus standing on a distant mountain. He asked me over and over and over, during each scene of the movie, 'At that time what did you do for your fellow man? At that time what did you do for your fellow man? At that time what did you do for your fellow man?' These were the most incredible, mind-blowing experiences I have ever had. We are absolutely our brothers' and sisters' keepers. The soul is much bigger than we know. The soul is huge."

These events result in tremendous positive consequences for those who have them. To reiterate, these people come to have no fear of death, an increase in belief in an afterlife and God, less emphasis on materialism, a more loving and joyful attitude along with a conviction that there is a wonderful afterlife that awaits all of us. The near death experience gives humanity a powerful, profound and hopeful message. These are not dreams or hallucinations, they are absolutely real events of Spirit. They are ineffable, incapable of being described in words.

Another woman gives her account. "I merged with and became one with the light. This was when the ecstasy and bliss started. The ecstasy was so intense and I knew that I was immortal, eternal, totally safe and had total knowledge. I had always existed, always would exist and all is well; there is a perfect plan that is working itself out in its perfection. I was like a receiver of immense Love and knowledge. I started to wonder how much more I could stand..."

"...the light then began to dissipate, I left the intensity and was in a green meadow. My personality was not any part of it. I felt unconditional Love, no judgment and total forgiveness. Punishment is not God's game. God is for us, not against us. Jesus raises our consciousness. There is no reason to fear death; it is the closing of one door and the opening of another. It will be wonderful to leave a worn-out body behind. This was a Spiritual dimension with total comprehension. We are so much more than we know, we are so unlimited. It is a great big universe/universes that we are a part of, we are part of God, the all of Love..."

"...I was able to look into my soul and know that my soul is total Love; everyone's soul is Love. I learned to know that there is no death. This was an enormous thing that happened to me; it is so much better than we think it is. I was in a meadow where the colors were unlike any colors I had ever seen before. I saw 18-20 people who seemed to be waiting for something and I met one man whose face was authoritative and beautiful; I knew I could trust him. He told me 'It is not time for you to be here yet'. I asked him what it was all about, what life was all about. He told me in a three sentence answer. Then he said that I could take the whole experience back except for the last answer. I would not be able to remember that answer..."

"...I knew that I had tapped into just the beginning of what there is to know. That it is a non-ending eternity which is all so much more vast than anything anyone could make up. Earth is one little way station to bring light and Love; a gift, a blessing and a responsibility. If there was one gift that I could give to everyone, it would be for everyone to have a near death experience. We would have a beautiful world where everyone would know that 'I too am part of God'."

151

We chose to be here at this time of great Spiritual awakening. Our collective consciousness is being raised to heights never before seen in recorded history. We are all heroes as we knew there would be difficult times, yet we still volunteered. Even though we will see somewhat difficult periods, remember to have times for joy and playfulness. This will allow for the easiest transitions for people during this Spiritual unfoldment. We are all connected in this multi-dimensional reality. Try to make life a little easier, a little better, a little more loving, a little more joyful, for your fellow man. The old is passing away. We are Spiritual beings on heroic journeys.

The NDE is clear, intense, coherent and results in lasting effects of a lifetime. The experience seems to be more than we can even imagine and most often happens as an awesome, mind-stretching experience after accidents, hospital stays and flat-lining of the brain. Both consciousness and perception are enhanced while at the same time there is no brain activity. People describe that they could do anything they wanted at the speed of thought. The blind see while in a NDE. Most say the English language does not encompass the sights, sounds and feelings they had. "So awesome that I can't put words together, as I could never imagine what I experienced."

A woman saw all encompassing light everywhere. "In the presence of God. Awesome. No book, article, movie or anything can describe God's power as it dissolves everything. The power is so immense that it is beyond power; total Love and total oneness. This was a 'rooftop experience' which has to be shared. There is no such thing as death. God is real."

Another woman had a motorcycle accident which resulted in a fractured skull, numerous broken bones in her head and a two week coma. She suffered excruciating pain to the point where she asked God to "take me". She lifted out of her body and all her pain was gone. She saw an ethereal body of a male angel and noticed that he shined from within. "He took my hand and I was at Peace. We flew out the window over the Pacific Ocean and I saw a funnel shaped object above me with a pinpoint of light at the far end. It was a portal to another dimension where there was no space or time. It's hard to find words-we arrived at the other end and I saw the living presence of a being of light..."

"...The being was all knowing, knew everything that was going to happen, all things that were or ever were going to be. This has to be God, perfect in every sense. I was angry at the Vietnam War and all the suffering. The Love kept coming and I was able to ask every question that I ever wanted answers for. Perfect answers and all ramifications came instantly to my head. How could I have forgotten what I knew all along? I understood everything. I was like a child being cradled as we (the Sacred being and myself) took off by the speed of thought around the universe. We went from star to star, everything was lit up in galaxies, supernovas and celestial beings. It felt like I was home. We went on a tour where I found everything to be radiant and alive, everything in the universe is alive..."

"...I went through a portal into a newly formed, central star and melted into perfect oneness. It was the quintessence of everything that will exist, one with God and with all things. A drop of water in Creation, I did not want to leave the indescribable ecstasy. It was a million times more intense than Earthly life, cosmic interconnectedness. Everything happens for a purpose, there is no chance to die and there is a greater, more magnificent universe. It's more real than physical life. That was real, this is a dream."

A woman had a tire blowout and ended up in an accident. The next she remembers, "Is being out of my body in the emergency room. I knew everything about everyone in the emergency room. I rose to the 2nd floor and I knew everything about everyone there. I raised out of the hospital and into space and thought, 'This is great!' The Milky Way was a few feet in front of me and I didn't know where I needed to go. I saw one faint star and was instantly there. I was welcomed by those who had passed and saw a blinding light, but I could look at it. I wondered why my life was so difficult and was told, 'Don't you remember you chose this?' Then I recalled choices I had made before birth..."

"...Now it was time for me to judge myself for actions during life. I regretted the actions I took which hurt others. Then I was given the choice to stay or leave. The doctor who worked on me said he would give up the profession if I died so I wanted him to remain a doctor. I went back. I had amnesia for months where I couldn't remember anything but the experience. I am dramatically changed because of this and realize that we are extensions of the Creator. I am now non-denominational, psychic, intuitive and a healer."

After reading the descriptions given by men, women and children of their experiences we must, if nothing else, be amazed at the glorious visions they saw. The world/realm that these souls were in is what the physical realm of Earthly life is in potentiality. When the Spiritual truths of unconditional Love and body/Spirit awareness become widely disseminated, then the people of Earth will create on Earth the type of world that mirrors the world/realm these people's souls experienced.

A man describes, "...the most profound experience of my life. In bed I had a seizure and was at risk of dying. It was the most fantastic, real event of my life, I was in a place where there was no place. I saw an envelope coalesce into an infinite ball of light that contained the universe. I could not wrap my mind around it and marveled at the ball of light, drew toward it. Then I had a life review which defined who I was, centering on areas of struggle. I began to feel on edge then, being enveloped by the non-judging, unconditional Love of the light. I began to dissolve into the infinite Love presence ..."

"...It was a timeless feeling. The light began to fade and I did not want to leave life. An awareness came that the phenomenal world was a fraction of the whole but still one. My mission is to communicate what I experienced as best I know to others. Third dimensional beliefs are inadequate to describe the light but it is infinite, the source of everything. The effects are the recognition of the incredible matrix and the dance of life. There is no separation. I have a deep desire to help others and serve. All of us are waking up to more than we see on the planet right now."

A woman had many near death experiences and describes one where she went with a friend to the light. "I had eye surgery when I was ten years old and was afraid I could not see. My parents went home and I was afraid when a nun walked in and told me to 'be a good girl'. I was outside of my body, could see, and met my friend Jimmy who asked me, 'Do you want to walk me home?' I said yes, he took my hand and we walked toward the light. Jimmy ran to his friends and family in the light, turned around and waved goodbye to me..."

"...I was back in my hospital bed and there were two angels with me. They told me that Jimmy was hit by a car in an accident and he died in the same hospital. Jimmy found me because I knew the way 'home' from a previous near-death experience. I am no longer afraid after the NDE. Love is for everybody. I have work yet to do here. When the work is done I'll walk home with Jimmy."

It is not by coincidence that the phenomenon of the near death experience is being learned of by more and more people on the planet. Their increased knowledge of Spiritual realms is contributing to the evolution of mankind's Spirit. As mentioned, the people who have had the experiences have been profoundly changed by them. They have been in direct contact with the world of the Spirit; the essence of all the universe. This phenomenon is of major importance regarding the increase of Spiritual knowledge and wisdom available to mankind.

Another woman had to go in to the hospital for a routine arthroscopic knee surgery. All of a sudden "I felt very cold. I woke up in the recovery room and overheard a commotion where the other patient in the room was. I remember thinking to myself that there was a lot going on there. The nurse spoke my name, then I realized they were talking to me! I was out of my body, looked at who I thought was my roommate and it was me. I felt no fear but I found myself floating to the corner of the room, looking down at me. I thought to myself 'How curious this is.' I felt no anxiety but I was mesmerized, not overwhelmed or terrified. Then an energy pulled me out and away from the recovery room to a place of blackness, I was being pushed into the blackness. I could feel myself becoming lighter and I was looking for something to hold onto. Then I saw a glimmer of light that began to grow as I looked at it..."

"...The light was encompassing and now it was pulling me toward it as it grew in size. I became overwhelmed by light everywhere and the feelings that came to me. I was floating through the light with its brilliance while feeling immense joy and an overwhelming ecstasy. I found myself floating between two rows of hooded beings and feeling cherished, unconditional Love and like I was coming home. The feelings went to the core of my being when one of the beings said, 'You have a child. You cannot stay.' This was a divine experience that I've never had in my life, so I answered, 'No! This is home. This is that bliss that I've always wanted.' 'You must go back. You have a child.'..."

"...I knew I had to go back and then I was instantaneously back in my body in the recovery room. I felt both changed and befuddled from the experience. There was no pain from the surgery and I healed extremely quickly; this was a gift. It took many years before I gained an understanding of the experience. My psychic abilities have been raised and I find it an amazing experience to help others remove blocks and connect with their hearts. There is no more judgment. Life is about joy and loving as Love is the only reality, there is nothing to be afraid of on the other side or in life. Seeing through the eyes of source equals unconditional Love..."

"...While having the NDE I was connected to everything. I had all the answers to everything with total clarity. Now I have a gentle awareness and understanding of the experience. We come into human form for the human qualities and challenges, we are God in human form, God experiencing God. Our ego wants us to separate from God for control and we come from our hearts/Spirits when we get rid of the ego. Maintaining our connection to source while remaining grounded is a challenge for all of us. Our Spirit speaks through us with Love and eliminates ego and negativity. It is important to know that we came in as Creators with an agenda. Trust with a leap of faith and always let your heart rule. Trust in life..."

"...The light is so much more than the sun. The light is alive with a feeling of Love and compassion. It contains a million fragments of all the souls that will be or will ever be in a

155

Love that is so overpowering and otherworldly. When do we reach out to the light? The times when we are challenged. I met light beings that welcomed me home and I knew them as family. They went through my life review with me. You look so closely at your life from the point of view of everyone you interact with as you feel their pain and joy. I learned how my actions affected others along with my future. There was no judgment as I had to relive actions that I had taken which caused me regret. The actions taken with a loving intention caused the biggest ripples, like ripples on a pond. We are to live with passion and loving intention. Consciousness lives on in pure form."

This increased Spiritual knowledge and wisdom can now be utilized and factored into the decisions human beings make both as individuals and collectively. On an individual basis the awareness of the consequences of our actions will reduce anger and its displays. When we understand that the other person will be hurt we will minimize or eliminate anger, hurtful words, physical violence and any other action which is harmful to another. We can only imagine what good changes with regard to large scale decisions and actions will come about when this Spiritual knowledge is taken into account.

The human race has created the conditions on Earth. There is no reason to believe that the human race cannot create more favorable conditions for itself. Who says that there cannot be a world created where Love, Peace, equity and justice are at the forefront in all considerations, whether on a personal, national or international level? Fortunately positive changes are happening on Mother Earth due to the increased communications between people of all nations over the world internet. You would probably agree that the Earth and her human residents have seen and experienced enough suffering.

Given the fearful information we have been given about life and death by certain religions the NDE would seem to negate the fear contained in some teachings. We are speaking of the fear induced upon humans concerning Heaven and hell being the only options at "death". Could the hellish experience be that which we experience here on Earth because of our lack of Spiritual awareness? The dominance of a person's ego could be seen as a form of hellish experience. The aspect of the life reviews where the person feels the pain of those who were hurt by them would seem to be a form of hell. Even those who get "get away" with crimes where others are hurt will be unable to escape a hellish guilt.

Adding to our dissatisfaction and sadness in this life is the state indicated by the being in Heaven asking the NDE'r, "What did you do for your fellow man?" Perhaps this aspect of life, helping your fellow man, explains the personal problems experienced by those who are considered rich and prosperous. We all must choose between the serving of self (ego) and the serving of others (Spirit). Those of us who chose to serve self will learn our lessons as we go to the Spirit. We will experience what those who crossed our paths during our lifetime felt, according to how we chose during those times. We will know whether we chose to serve self or serve others during our life reviews and learn Spiritual lessons.

The life review is something that we can understand because we have all experienced regret after hurting others. We have all experienced regret in situations where we did not take the actions which could have helped others. The extreme example here is where the other who we failed to help passes on. These regrets are the most painful as there is not any way to correct the omissions or apologize. It would seem, if any of you have experienced this extreme example, that you should not allow yourself to be too upset about your regrets as the soul of your departed Loved one fully understands from the realm of Spirit.

All we can do is our best in this life. When we become more and more spiritually aware we will take the actions which will help those who we come into contact with. We will not hesitate to be honest with our Loved ones so that there will be no regrets. We will not hesitate to take those actions which will result in improvements in the lives of our fellow brothers and sisters in the family of man. There will come the time where we will do no harm to any living thing, as all will be seen as one. We will understand that if we harm others we are only harming ourselves.

Once this Spiritual awareness and wisdom reaches everyone on the planet Earth there will be an elimination of all harmful acts. In all areas of life actions taken will be for the uplifting of life. Those actions which are harmful to life will diminish to the point where they will be non-existent. What we are describing is a Heaven on Earth. The realm which those who experienced the near death experience went to will be exactly the same as the physical realm. Ask yourself if this is possible. Not only is this transformation of life on Earth to a Heavenly realm possible it is the inevitable, final end result of human Spiritual evolution.

Bodhisattvas are souls of great enlightenment who, according to Buddhism, postpone/forego nirvana in order to bring enlightenment to the entire, suffering human race as well as all sentient beings. One would have to believe, given the rapid Spiritual evolution humans are experiencing at this time, that many bodhisattvas are here helping with total enlightenment. You will find them all around the planet giving wisdom to the world for the purpose of Spiritual enlightenment. The changes happening on Earth at this time are coming with the help of these bodhisattvas and are evidenced by the Spiritually mature movements and

157

ideas of millions.

It is extremely encouraging to see the Spiritual evolution of the human race occur. As more and more find wisdom the world situation is improving exponentially day by day. We express gratitude that these magnificent, positive changes are happening and that the enlightenment of all is approaching. Humanity is ready to reach the highest of heights.

A Native American Prayer.

"So live your life that the fear of death can never enter your heart. Trouble no one about their religion; respect others in their view, and demand that they respect yours. Love your life, perfect your life, beautify all things in your life. Seek to make your life long and its purpose in the service of your people. Prepare a noble death song for the day when you go over the great divide. Always give a sign of salute when meeting or passing a friend, even a stranger, when in a lonely place..."

"...Show respect to all people and grovel to none. When you arise in the morning give thanks for the food and for the joy of living. If you see no reason for giving thanks, the fault lies only with yourself. Abuse no one and nothing, for abuse turns the wise ones to fools and robs the Spirit of its vision. When it comes your time to die, be not like those whose hearts are filled with the fear of death, so that when their time comes they weep and pray for a little more time to live their lives over again in a different way. Sing your death song and die like a hero going home."

Feel the feeling of Heaven on Earth. Thank the Creator that you are witnessing these magnificent events with your very eyes. Humanity's future is profoundly bright. Thank you.

Notes

Selected Quotes.

It is our hope that these thoughts comfort, stimulate and challenge you. If the reading of these words results in an improvement of the conditions in the life of one human being then we can rejoice.

Benjamin Franklin (1706-1790)

"There seem to be but three ways for a nation to acquire wealth: the first is by war, as the Romans did, in plundering their conquered neighbors-this is robbery; the second by commerce, which is generally cheating; the third by agriculture, the only honest way, wherein man received a real increase of the seed thrown into the ground, in a kind of continual miracle, wrought by the hand of God in his favor, as a reward for his innocent life and his virtuous industry."

Sigmund Freud (1856-1939)

"As regards intellectual work, it remains a fact, indeed, that great decisions in the realms of thought and momentous discoveries and solutions of problems are only possible to an individual, working in solitude."

Thomas Fuller (1654-1734)

"The pleasures of the rich are bought with the tears of the poor."

Henry George (1839-1897)

"There are three ways by which an individual can get wealthy-by work, by gift, and by theft. And, clearly, the reason why the workers get so little is that the beggars and thieves get so much."

Josiah William Gitt (1884-1973)

"Humanity's most valuable assets have been the non-conformists. Were it not for the non-conformists, he who refuses to go along with the continuance of things as they are, and insists upon attempting to find new ways of bettering things, the world would have known little progress indeed."

Horace (65-8 B.C.)

"Who then is free? The wise man, who is lord over himself, whom neither poverty, or death, nor bonds affright, who bravely defies his passions, and scorns ambition, who in himself is a whole, smoothed and rounded, so that nothing outside can rest on the polished surface, and against whom fortune in her onset is ever defeated."

Aldous Huxley (1894-1963)

"That men do not learn from the lessons of history is the most important of all the lessons of history."

I Ching or "Book of Changes" (12th century B.C.)

"But when two people are at one in their inmost hearts, they shatter even the strength of iron or of bronze. And when two people understand each other in their inmost hearts, their words are sweet and strong, like the fragrance of orchids."

Robert Ingersoll (1833-1899)

"The object of the freethinker is to ascertain the truth-the conditions of well-being-to the end that his life will be made of value."

Thomas Jefferson (1743-1826)

"Experience declares that man is the only animal which devours his own kind; for i can apply no milder term to the governments of europe, and to the general prey of the rich on the poor."

Carl Gustav Jung (1875-1961)

"What is essential in the work of art is that it should rise far above the realm of personal life and speak from the Spirit and heart of mankind. The personal aspect is a limitation-and even a sin-in the realm of art. When a form of 'art' is primarily personal it deserves to be treated as if it were a neurosis... Art is a kind of innate drive that seizes a human being and makes him its instrument. The artist is not a person endowed with free will who seeks his own ends, but one who allows art to realize its purpose through him. As a human being he may have moods and a will and personal aims, but as an artist he is 'man' in a higher sense-he is 'collective man'-one who carries and shapes the unconscious, psychic forms of mankind."

Kabir (1400-1499)

"Men have always looked before and after, and rebelled against the existing order. But for their divine discontent men would not have been men, and there would have been no progress in human affairs."

Nikos Kazantzakis (1883-1957)

"It is not God who will save us, it is we who will save God-by battling, by creating, and by transmuting matter into Spirit."

Helen Keller (1880-1968)

"The country is governed for the richest, for the corporations, the bankers, the land speculators, and for the exploiters."

John Maynard Keynes (1883-1946)

"When the accumulation of wealth is no longer of high social importance, there will be great changes in the code of morals. We shall be able to rid ourselves of many of the pseudo-moral principles which have hag-ridden us for two hundred years, by which we have exalted some of the most distasteful of human qualities into the position of highest virtues."

Archibald Macleish (1892-1982)

"The dissenter is every human being at those moments of his life when he resigns momentarily from the herd and thinks for himself."

James Madison (1751-1836)

"If there be a principle that ought not to be questioned in the United States, it is that every man has a right to abolish an old government and establish a new one. This principle is not only recorded in every public archive, written in every American heart, and sealed with the blood of a host of American martyrs, but is the only lawful tenure by which the United States hold their existence as a nation."

Marcus Aurelius Antonius (121-180 A.D.)

"And thou wilt give thyself relief, if thou doest every act of thy life as if it were the last, laying aside all carelessness and passionate aversion from the commands of reason, and all hypocrisy, and self-Love, and discontent with all the portion which has been given to thee."

H.L. Mencken (1880-1956)

"But any man who afflicts the human race with ideas must be prepared to see them misunderstood, and that is what happened to Jesus."

Henry Miller (1891-1980)

"For some reason or other man looks for the miracle, and to accomplish it he will wade through blood. He will debauch himself with ideas, he will reduce himself to a shadow if for only one second of his life he can close his eyes to the hideousness of reality. Everything is endured-disgrace, humiliation, poverty, war, crime, boredom-in the belief that overnight something will occur, a miracle, which will render life tolerable... If now and then we encounter pages that explode, pages that wound and sear, that wring groans and tears and curses, know that they come from a man with his back up, a man whose only defenses left are his words and his words are always stronger than the lying, crushing weight of the world, stronger than all the racks and wheels which the cowardly invent to crush out the miracle of personality... The task which the artist implicitly sets himself is to overthrow existing values, to make of the chaos about him an order which is his own, to sow strife and ferment so that by the emotional release those who are dead may be restored to life."

Robert Oppenheimer (1904-1967)

"There must be no barriers for freedom in inquiry. There is no place for dogma in science. The scientist is free, and must be free to ask any question, to doubt any assertion, to seek for any evidence, to correct any errors."

George Orwell (1903-1950)

"I think there are four great motives for writing... (1) Sheer egoism. Desire to seem clever, to be talked about, to be remembered after death, to get your own back on grown-ups who snubbed you in childhood, etc.... (2) Aesthetic enthusiasm... (3) Historical impulse. Desire to see things as they are, to find out true facts and store them up for posterity. (4) Political purpose-using the word 'political' in the widest possible sense. Desire to push the world in a certain direction, to alter other people's idea of the kind of society that they should strive after."

Thomas Paine (1737-1809)

"It is wrong to say that God made rich and poor; he made only male and female; and he gave them the Earth for their inheritance... The Earth, in its natural uncultivated state was, and ever would have continued to be, the common property of the human race."

John Ruskin (1819-1900)

"The simplest and most necessary truths are always the last to be believed."

Antoine de Saint-Exupery (1900-1944)

"Let a man in a garret but burn with enough intensity and he will set fire to the whole world... I know of but one freedom and that is the freedom of the mind."

Harlow Shapley (1885-1972)

"That our planet is the one and only planet where life has emerged would be a ridiculous assumption... Even if only one in a hundred of the ten billion suitable planets has actually got life well under way, there would be more than 100 million such planets. No, it is presumptuous to think that we are alone."

Albert Camus (1913-1960)

"In all circumstances of life, the writer can recapture the feelings of a living community that will justify him. But only if he accepts as completely as possible the two trusts that constitute the nobility of his calling: the service of truth and the service of freedom."

Mohandes Gandhi (1869-1948)

"Life and death are but phases of the same thing, the reverse and obverse of the same coin... I want you all to treasure death and suffering more than life and to appreciate their cleansing and purifying character... Death which is an eternal verity is revolution, as birth and after is slow and steady evolution. Death is as necessary for man's growth as life itself."

Henry George (1839-1897)

"So long as all the increased wealth which modern progress brings goes but to build up great fortunes, to increase luxury and make sharper the contrast between the house of have and the house of want, progress is not real and cannot be permanent."

Maksim Gorki (1868-1936)

"And if it is thought necessary to speak of Sacred things, then the one Sacred thing is the dissatisfaction of man with himself and his striving to be better than he is; Sacred is his hatred of all the trivial rubbish he himself has created; Sacred is his desire to do away with greed, envy, crime, disease, war, and all enmity between man on Earth; and Sacred is his labor."

Horace Greeley (1811-1872)

"But the world does move, and its motive power under God is the fearless thought and speech of those who dare to be in advance of their time-who are sneered at and shunned through their days of struggle as lunatics, dreamers, impracticables and visionaries; men of crochets, vagaries and isms."

Ernest Hemingway (1898-1961)

"For fascism is a lie told by bullies. A writer who will not lie cannot live or work under fascism. Because fascism is a lie, it is condemned to literary sterility. And when it is past, it will have no history, except the bloody history of murder."

William James (1842-1910)

"Without any exception known to me, militarist authors take a highly mystical view of their subject, and regard war as a biological or sociological necessity, uncontrolled by ordinary psychological checks and motives. When the time of development is ripe the war must come, reason or no reason, for the justifications pleaded are invariably fictitious. War is, in short, a permanent human obligation... I devoutly believe in the reign of Peace and in the gradual advent of some sort of socialistic equilibrium. The fatalistic view of the war-function is to me nonsense... And when whole nations are the armies, and the science of destruction vies in intellectual refinement with the sciences of production, I see that war becomes absurd and impossible from its own monstrosity."

Lao-Tzu (c. 565 B.C.)

"In time of war men, civilized in Peace, turn from their higher to their lower nature. But triumph is not beautiful. He who thinks a triumph beautiful is one with a will to kill. The death of a multitude is cause for mourning. Conduct your triumph as a funeral."

Pierre Sylvain Marechal (1750-1803)

"Let the revolting distinction of rich and poor disappear, once and for all, the distinction of great and small, of masters and valets, of governors and governed. Let there be no difference between human beings other than those of age and sex. Since all have the same needs and the same faculties, let there be one education for all, one food for all."

James Mill (1773-1836)

"The positions which we have already established with regard to human nature, and which we assume as foundations, are these: that the actions of men are governed by their wills, and their wills by their desires; that their desires are directed to pleasure and relief from pain as ends, and that wealth and power as the principal means; that to the desire of these means there is no limit; and that the actions which flow from this unlimited desire are the constituents whereof bad government is made."

John Stuart Mill (1806-1873)

"If all mankind minus one were of one opinion, and only one person were of the contrary opinion, mankind would be no more justified in silencing that one person, than he, if he had the power, would be justified in silencing mankind... But the peculiar evil of silencing the expression of an opinion is, that it is robbing the human race; posterity as well as the existing generation; those who dissent from the opinion, still more from those who hold it. If the opinion is right, they are deprived of the opportunity of exchanging error for truth; if wrong, they lose, what is always as great a benefit, the clearer perception and livelier impression of truth, produced by its collision with error."

Robert Millikan (1868-1953)

"There are only two kinds of immoral conduct. The first is due to indifference, thoughtlessness, failure to reflect on what is for the common good. The second type of immorality is represented by 'the unpardonable sin' of which Jesus spoke-deliberate refusal, after reflection, to follow the light when seen."

Linus Pauling (1901-1994)

"Man has reached his present state through the process of evolution. The last great step in evolution was the mutational process that doubled the size of the brain, about one million years ago; this led to the origin of man. It is this change in the brain that permits the inheritance of acquired characteristics of a certain sort-the inheritance of knowledge, of learning, through communication from one human being to another... Man's great power of thinking, remembering, and communicating are responsible for the evolution of civilization."

Plato (428-348 B.C.)

"A man must take with him into the world below an adamantine faith in truth and right, that there too he may be un-dazzled by the desire of wealth or other allurements of evil, lest coming upon tyrannies and similar villainies, he should do irremediable wrongs to others and suffer yet worse himself; but let him know how to choose the mean and avoid extremes on either side, as far as possible, not only in this life, but in all that is to come. For this is the way to happiness."

"Whence come wars and fightings, and factions? Whence but from the body and the lusts of the body? Wars are occasioned by the Love of money, and money has to be acquired for the same and service of the body."

Red Jacket (1758-1830)

"You have got our country, but are not satisfied; you want to force your religion upon us... Brother, you say there is but one way to worship and serve the Great Spirit. If there is but one religion, why do you white people differ so much about it?"

Jean Jacques Rousseau (1712-1778)

"The first man who, having enclosed a piece of ground, bethought himself of saying, 'this is mine', and found people simple enough to believe him, was the real founder of civil society. From how many crimes, wars and murders, from how many horrors and misfortunes might not anyone have saved mankind by pulling up the stakes, or filling up the ditch, and crying to his fellows, 'Beware of listening to this imposter; you are undone if you once forget that the fruits of the Earth belong to us all, and the Earth itself to nobody."

Andrei Sakharov (1921-1989)

"Intellectual freedom is essential to human society... Freedom of thought is the only guarantee against an infection of people by mass myths, which, in the hands of treacherous hypocrites and demagogues, can be transformed into bloody dictatorships."

Arthur Schopenhauer (1778-1860)

"But life is short and truth works far and lives long: let us speak the truth."

"No difference of rank, position, or birth, is so great as the gulf which separates the countless millions who use their head only in the service of their belly, in other words, look upon it as an instrument of the will, and those very few and rare persons who have the courage to say: No! It is too good for that, my head shall be active in its own service; it shall try to comprehend the wondrous and varied spectacle of this world, and then reproduce it in some form, whether as art or as literature, that may answer to my character as an individual."

B.F. Skinner (1904-1990)

"Better contraceptives will control population only if people will use them. A nuclear holocaust can be prevented only if the conditions under which nations make war can be changed. The environment will continue to deteriorate until pollution practices are abandoned. We need to make vast changes in human behavior."

Leon Uris (1924-2003)

"To me a writer is one of the most important soldiers in the fight for the survival of the human race. He must stay at his post in the thick of fire to serve the cause of mankind."

Chief Red Cloud (1822-1909)

"You must begin anew and put away the wisdom of your fathers. You must lay up food and forget the hungry. When your house is built, your storeroom filled, then look around for a neighbor whom you can take advantage of and seize all he has."

Chief Sitting Bull (1831-1890)

"...Because I am a red man. If the Great Spirit had desired me to be a white man he would have made me so in the first place. He put in your heart certain wishes and plans, in my heart he put other and different desires. Each man is good in his sight. It is not necessary for eagles to be crows."

Rolling Thunder (1916-1997)

"The most basic principle of all is that of not harming others, and that includes all people and all life and all things. It means not controlling or manipulating others, not trying to manage their affairs. It means not going off to some other land and killing people over there- not for religion or politics or military exercises or any other excuse. No being has the right to harm or control any other being. No individual or government has the right to force others to join or participate in any group or system or to force others to go to school, to church or to war. Every being has the right to live his own life in his own way."

"Every being has an identity and a purpose. To live up to his purpose, every being has the power of self-control, and that's where Spiritual power begins. When some of these fundamental things are learned, the time will be right for more to be revealed and Spiritual power will come again to this land."

Buddha (c. 563-483 B.C.)

"This is the noble eightfold way: namely, right view, right intention, right speech, right action, right livelihood, right effort, right mindfulness, right concentration. This, monks, is the middle path, of which the taghagata has gained enlightment, which produces insight and knowledge, and tends to calm, to higher knowledge, enlightment, nirvana."

'Now this, monks, is the noble truth of the cause of pain: the craving, which tends to rebirth, combined with pleasure and lust, finding pleasure here and there; namely, the craving for passion, the craving for existence, the craving for nonexistence."

Confucius (551-479 B.C.)

"Sincerity is the way of heaven. The attainment of sincerity is the way of men. He who possesses sincerity, is he who, without an effort, hit what is right, and apprehends, without the exercise of thought; he is the sage who naturally and easily embodies the right way. He who attains to sincerity, is he who chooses what is good, and firmly holds it fast."

Mohandes Gandhi (1869-1948)

"I believe in the doctrine of non-violence as a weapon of the weak. I believe in the doctrine of non-violence as a weapon of the strongest. I believe that a man is the strongest soldier for daring to die unarmed."

Albert Schweitzer (1875-1965)

"A man is truly ethical only when he obeys the compulsion to help all life which he is able to assist, and shrinks from injuring anything that lives."

Percy Shelley (1792-1822)

"Fear not that the tyrants shall rule forever,

Or the priests of the bloody faith;

They stand on the brink of the mighty river

Whose waves they have tainted with death:...

And their swords and their scepters I floating see

Like wrecks, on the surge of eternity."

Alexander Solzhenitsyn (1918-2008)

"The simple act of any ordinary courageous man is not to take part, not to support lies!... Writers and artists can do more: they can vanquish lies! In the struggle against lies, art has always won and always will... Lies can stand up against much in the world, but not against art."

Henry David Thoreau (1817-1862)

"If Christ should appear on Earth he would on all hands be denounced as a mistaken, misguided man, insane and crazed."

Leo Tolstoy (1828-1910)

"All men know in their very earliest years that beside the good of their animal personality, there is another, a better, a good in life, which is not only independent of the gratification of the appetites of the animal personality, but on the contrary, the greater the renunciation of the welfare of the animal personality the greater the good becomes... This feeling... Is known to all. This feeling is Love."

"Freethinkers are those who are willing to use their minds without prejudice and without fearing to understand things that clash with their own customs, privileges, or beliefs. This state of mind is not common, but it is essential for right thinking; where it is absent, discussion is apt to become worse than useless."

Voltaire (1694-1778)

"All the philosophers of the world who had a religion have said in all ages: 'There is a God; and one must be just'. That, then is the universal religion established in all ages and throughout mankind. The point in which they all agree is therefore true, and the systems through which they differ therefore false."

Chief Seattle (1780-1866)

"It matters little where we pass the remnants of our days. They will not be many. A few more moons; a few more winters-and not one of the descendants of the mighty hosts that once moved over this broad land or lived in happy homes, protected by the Great Spirit, will remain to mourn over the graves of a people once more powerful and hopeful than yours. But why should I mourn at the untimely fate of my people? Tribe follows tribe, nation follows nation, like the waves of the sea. It is the order of nature, and regret is useless. Your time of decay may be distant, but it will surely come, for even the white man whose God walked and talked with him as friend with friend, cannot be exempted from the common destiny. We may be brothers after all. We shall see."

"To us the ashes of our ancestors are Sacred and their resting place is hallowed ground. You wander far from the graves of your ancestors and seemingly without regret... Your dead cease to Love you and the land of their nativity as soon as they pass the portals of the tomb and wander away beyond the stars. They are soon forgotten and never return. Our dead never forget the beautiful world that gave them being..."

"Every part of this soil is Sacred in the estimation of my people. Every hillside, every valley, every plain and grove, has been hallowed by some sad or happy event in days long vanished. The very dust upon which you now stand responds more lovingly to their footsteps than to yours, because it is rich with the blood of our ancestors and our bare feet are conscious of the sympathetic touch. Even the little children who lived here and rejoiced here for a brief season will Love these somber solitudes and at eventide they greet shadowy returning Spirits. And when the last red man shall have perished, and the memory of my tribe shall have become a myth among the white men, these shores will swarm with the invisible dead of my tribe, and when your children's children think themselves alone in the field, the store, the shop, upon the highway, or in the silence of the pathless woods, they will not be alone. At night when the streets of your cities and villages are silent and you think they are deserted, they will throng with the returning hosts that once filled and still Love this beautiful land. The white man will never be alone. Let him be just and deal kindly with my people, for the dead are not powerless. Dead, did I say? There is no death, only a change of worlds."

Rolling Thunder (1916-1997)

"Modern man talks of harnessing nature, conquering nature and making nature a servant of man. This shows that modern man doesn't know the first thing about nature and nature's ways. And the condition of the environment today proves that. Now everyone's afraid-afraid of air pollution, radioactivity and poisoned water. The land is becoming contaminated and the resources are disappearing or becoming unusable, and now people wonder if it's too late. You can't make any kind of laws or system to control nature or to control man's inner nature, his consciousness or his natural behavior-the way he thinks and feels. That cannot be controlled. No individual or group can block another individual's path or change it against what fits his nature and his purpose. It might be done for a time, but in the end it won't work out. It will only lead to danger and fear for everyone. Even in healing we take that into account. A true healer considers a man's karma and his destiny. He has a way of looking into and understanding what is meant to be according to each individual's own progress and unfoldment. That way things are more realistic and it saves everyone a lot of trouble. Nature is sovereign and man's inner nature is sovereign. Nature is to be respected. All life and every single living being is to be respected. That's the only answer."

"Back in Oklahoma some years ago, there was a meeting-the first such high level meeting in over a hundred years-where chiefs and medicine men came together from all over the continent, and some from South America. The Iroquois came from New York and they brought a board with writing on it. On the last day of the ceremonies we formed a huge circle."

"The circle is the Great Spirit's emblem. All life is a circle. The world is a circle and the atoms are circles. The circle is seen on the rock writings, and it goes around all things, it takes in all things. When we met in Oklahoma, we formed a huge circle of all native tribes and we smoked the Peace pipe to the sun, and it stayed lit around that huge circle. Then the Iroquois brought out the board with writing on it and interpreted it. They said 'today our tribes are united again'. The emblem showed a chain of hands-people holding hands in a circle-and they said 'today our people have formed the circle of brotherhood and friendship here'."

"Eventually, this circle will go around the world. The brotherhood and Peace that the world is seeking will now start on this land here. All the people here will be joined in the circle of friendship and brotherhood and that circle will go around the world."

We would like to thank you for taking the time to read this work. We hope that you have been blessed and benefitted by doing so. Our prayer is that the benefits you have received will be shared with others and that they too will share with others. Then the circle of friendship and brotherhood will go around the world. Thank you.

Notes

Finale.

W. Somerset Maugham

"The great tragedy of life is not that men perish, but that they cease to Love."

After all of our experiences as human beings, there is no doubt that our lives have a meaning and a purpose. Philosophers from time immemorial have thought deeply about the meaning of life. What is life all about? What conclusions can we arrive at? Can we arrive at a place where we can be reasonably certain that we have arrived at truth? We have seen in Part Two of this work, The Spiritual Realm, some very powerful truths.

Isadora Duncan

"Art is not necessary at all. All that is necessary to make this world a better place to live in is to Love-to Love as Christ Loved, as Buddha Loved."

The empathy conveyed by all of the true artists and the true people throughout history is the essence of the reality of life. This is that feeling which comes to those who have first cried. The true people cry for their fellow brothers and sisters who experience suffering, as we all suffer. The coming to the conclusion that we are all the same and one is the ultimate realization which brings us to truth.

Ralph Waldo Emerson

"The power of Love, as the basis of a state, has never been tried... There will always be a government of force where men are selfish..."

The truth is Love is all there is to be concerned about. The eventual conclusion that we all come to know occurs when we understand the truth of Love. There is no higher truth than Love. Love is the reason for our being. How can one express Love in such a way that the importance of Love is not misunderstood, not diminished and given expression equal to its unparalleled force and power? How can one explain Love? The simple mention of the word Love confirms the absolute power of this force.

Thomas Carlyle

"Love is ever the beginning of knowledge as fire is of light."

One who feels and understands the power of Love will see the suffering and hurt of others as a call to action in order to end that suffering and hurt. This is why an alternate title for this work was "First, Cry". We have the capacity as human beings to cry. "First, Cry" is the call to humanity to understand that when you come to a point where you are so moved that you cry this is extremely important. It is so important that you can safely say, that when you are moved to tears, that you are arriving at life's meaning.

Fyodor Dostoyevski

"Love a man even in his sin for that Love is a likeness of the divine Love, and is the summit of Love on Earth."

We arrive at this point of crying because we are so moved by absolute truth. One who cries is at that point where they have felt and understood the reality of life. So what do we do next? We risk our lives in order to spread the truth. The reality of the reason for our physical realm existence is to become Love. We have all had Loved ones die so we are all aware of death. There is no such thing as death; we are Spiritual beings and we are forever. We are in the physical realm in order to help save the human race.

There is no doubt that this thing we are experiencing called life will end. So let us go as far as we can go to understand life's meaning. Let us now leave no stone unturned. Looking on genetically modified food, the international financial system, war and the rest of the problems humanity suffers in the physical realm, we have the responsibility to make sense of it all.

Jesus Christ

"The kingdom of God is within you."

We are going to make the attempt to understand. We are going to attempt with all of our might to get to the reality of life's purpose. Why? Because whatever our personal philosophy, there is a reason for our existence in the physical realm. We have come to the point where we firmly believe that the truth of this existence is all about Love. Can anyone argue that if everyone on Earth had Love as their motivation at all times, that there could be no higher state for mankind? Think about Love and there is no other conclusion we can come to but that it is mankind's highest state.

Jesus Christ

"Even the least among you can do all that I have done, and greater things."

We as humans have the ability to place Love at the forefront of our every action. This is what life means; Love is our essence. Life is an unbelievably beautiful experience. If we can look at things from the perspective of what we are going to be experiencing after this life, then we are left with no alternative but to move toward ultimate truth. We have come to the awareness that this life will end. As there is no doubt that our physical body will end, the question must be asked.

Jesus Christ

"This is my commandment, that you Love one another, even as I have Loved you."

What are we to do with our bodies and our lives? If one were to be totally honest the answer to the question is to give and receive Love. Think seriously about the fact that everyone you meet is going to die. We are trying to understand the reasons why we as human beings are dealing with genetically modified food, the global financial system, war, greed, poverty, starvation, environmental degradation and all of our other problems.

Jesus Christ

"Greater Love hath no man than this, that one lay down his life for his friends."

What would happen if every man, woman and child on Earth attained Christ consciousness? Take a few minutes here to imagine what this world would look like.

Please do take a short time now and imagine that this human condition has become an actual reality.

After imagining humanity in that state where all have attained Christ consciousness, you have seen mankind's true potential....   Heaven.

Notes

Notes

www.ingramcontent.com/pod-product-compliance
Lightning Source LLC
Chambersburg PA
CBHW082133290526
45794CB00008B/3019